BACKROADS

—— *of* ——

SOUTHERN

CALIFORNIA

BACKROADS

—— *of* ——

SOUTHERN
CALIFORNIA

*Your Guide to Southern California's
Most Scenic Backroad Adventures*

Text and Photography by David M. Wyman

Voyageur Press

A Pictorial
Discovery Guide

Edited by Danielle J. Ibister
Designed by Maria Friedrich
Maps by Mary Firth
Printed in China

05   06   07   08   09   5   4   3   2   1

Library of Congress Cataloging-in-Publication Data

Wyman, David M., 1948-
Backroads of southern California : your guide to southern California's most scenic backroad adventures /
text and photography by David M. Wyman.
     p. cm. — (A pictorial discovery guide)
Includes bibliographical references (p.   ) and index.
ISBN 0-89658-058-X (pbk. : alk. paper)
1. Automobile travel—California, Southern—Guidebooks. 2. Scenic byways—California, Southern—Guidebooks.
3. California, Southern—Tours. 4. California, Southern—Pictorial works. I. Title. II. Series.

  F867.W96 2005
  917.94'90454—dc22
                                    2005001343

Published by Voyageur Press, Inc.
123 North Second Street, P.O. Box 338, Stillwater, MN 55082 U.S.A.
651-430-2210, fax 651-430-2211
books@voyageurpress.com
www.voyageurpress.com

Educators, fundraisers, premium and gift buyers, publicists, and marketing managers: Looking for creative products and new sales ideas? Voyageur Press books are available at special discounts when purchased in quantities, and special editions can be created to your specifications. For details contact the marketing department at 800-888-9653.

TITLE PAGE:
The coastline of Montana de Oro State Park alternates between inviting beaches and rugged promontories.

TITLE PAGE, INSET:
Bright poppies add color to the Carrizo Plain.

CONTENTS

INTRODUCTION

In the mid nineteenth century, anyone traveling north from Los Angeles over Sepulveda Pass in the Santa Monica Mountains would have been rewarded with a fine view of rural San Fernando Valley. As a child during the mid-twentieth century, I sometimes crossed the same pass on a two-lane road in the company of my parents, brother, and the dog in the family car. To me, the route over the pass was a backroad, although our view of the San Fernando Valley over the years included a dwindling patchwork of farms and ranches interspersed among a growing design of housing tracts.

Now, in the twenty-first century, an eight-lane freeway traverses Sepulveda Pass. The San Fernando Valley has more housing tracts and a bumper crop of office buildings along broad thoroughfares; the farms and ranches have almost disappeared. Given similar changes across California, I am not surprised when people ask me if there are any backroads left to explore in the southern half of the Golden State. My questioners are often surprised when I enthusiastically affirm that, when it comes to backroads, Southern California has an embarrassment of riches.

Despite the influx of people who began arriving in earnest with the gold rush of 1848, and the millions more who arrived after the end of World War II, there simply hasn't been enough time to fill all of the enor-

FACING PAGE:
A cross-country skier makes his way past giant sequoias and ponderosa pines in the southern Sierra Nevada.

ABOVE:
Wildflowers vie for attention with the boulder field at the Jumbo Rocks campground in Joshua Tree National Park.

mous open spaces in Southern California. In addition, the state and federal governments have protected millions of acres from development. In many places, the rugged nature of the land itself has held development in check.

I have met many who, before coming to Southern California, imagined that most of the land would be flat. It is true that much of the San Joaquin Valley barely rises above sea level. But California, north and south, is as vertical as it is horizontal, with an average elevation of almost three thousand feet. Southern California, rising in places from an elevation below the level of the sea to more than fourteen thousand feet above it, has been shaped for millions of years by powerful, sometimes violent, geological forces. Those forces still shape the mountains, deserts, and seacoast.

Some otherwise rational people claim that Southern California ends at the northern border of Los Angeles. Their desire to disassociate themselves from the southernmost regions of the state may lie more with perceived cultural differences than with geographical reality. In truth, the east-west centerline of the state is more than two hundred miles north of Los Angeles. That line runs east from the Pacific Ocean near the city of Santa Cruz, across the Coast Range Mountains and over the San Joaquin Valley to the city of Fresno, up and over the Sierra Nevada Range, and ends in the desert at the Nevada border. I have hewn to that line in this book and included as well backroads that lie to the east and south of the cities of Los Angeles and San Diego. These are backroads that travel close to the borders with Arizona and Mexico.

This book is organized into six relatively distinct geographical regions. The first region includes the roads of the Transverse Ranges. Some of these roads are surprisingly close to or even within the city limits of Los Angeles, while others travel beneath wild snow-clad peaks and circle the home range of the condor, the largest flying animal in North America. The backroads of the Central Coast travel to beaches, a lost city, a colony of giant seals, and a remote community that may well deserve the title of earthquake capital of the world. The San Joaquin Valley is the nation's agricultural powerhouse, produces much of the nation's oil, and has

seen the birth of social movements important to the history of the United States.

Roads in the superlative Sierra Nevada Range, the longest unbroken chain of mountains in North America, lead to views of the highest peak in the lower forty-eight states and to groves of sequoia trees, the largest living things on earth. The Mojave Desert counts among its attractions two national parks, the lowest point in the Western Hemisphere, the oldest living thing on earth, giant sand dunes, tiny fish, and a bizarre bush that looks like a tree. Finally, the sparely populated southern deserts and mountains are redolent with the history of American Indians, Spanish explorers and friars, and the settlers who followed them.

The backroads described in this book are mostly two-lane and paved, with all of them accessible to the average passenger car. Intrepid, well-conditioned bicycle riders could navigate most if not all of these roads, too; I've pedaled over a few of them myself. I have tried to find backroads that are not likely to be turned into multi-lane highways now or even in the far future, where the sound bulldozers and wrecking balls is at best indistinct, where the speed limit is fifty-five miles per hour or less, and where the road signs point away from the cities.

I have traveled all the backroads described in this book and more. Because I visited many remote places, I always carried a spare tire, a foot pump, and a first-aid kit. I also traveled with the *California Road Atlas and Driver's Guide*, published by Thomas Brothers. The Automobile Association of America (AAA) provided me with county and regional maps, while National Park and National Forest Service maps showed me the way on unpaved roads. On the local level, I picked up several chamber of commerce maps.

Sometimes I stayed in motels, and I spent a fair number of nights in a sleeping bag, usually under the stars, because rain is a relatively infrequent visitor to Southern California.

The reader will not need a motel reservation or a sleeping bag to explore the pages of this book. It is only necessary to pack a sense of adventure. Let's find a pass to cross, and together we'll travel the backroads of Southern California.

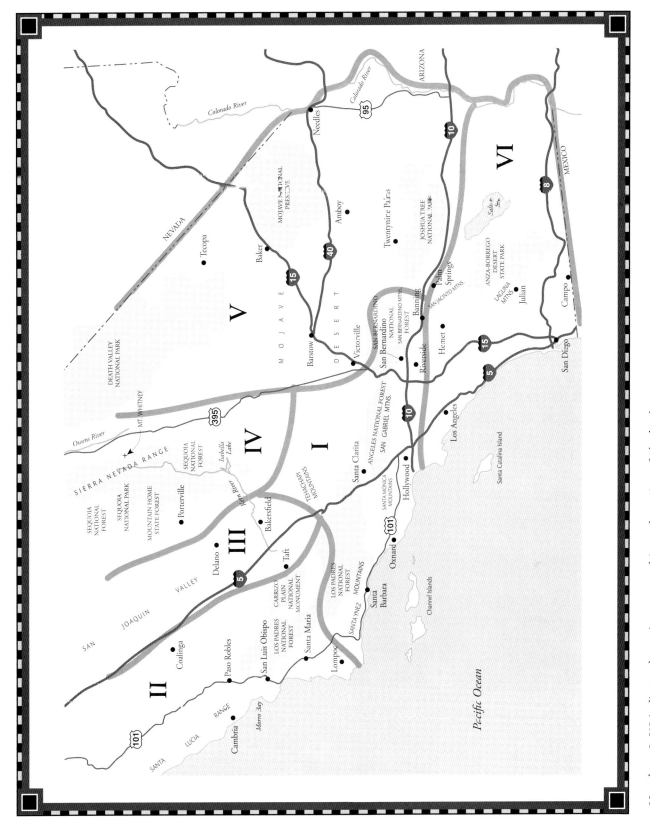

Numbers I–VI indicate the regions covered in each section of the book.

PART I

THE
TRANSVERSE RANGES

FACING PAGE:
The Ridge Route travels into the La Liebre Mountains past blooming wild mustard.

ABOVE:
This little, unnamed lake lies along the Gorman Post Road, at the base of the Tehachapi Mountains. It was created by movements of the earth along the San Andreas earthfault zone.

For more than three million years, powerful forces have been at work lifting the Transverse Ranges thousands of feet in elevation. Unusual in North America, the Transverse Ranges lie on an east-west axis, forming a barrier between the Los Angeles Basin and the northern part of the state. It's difficult to appreciate how much open space exists in these mountains that are so close to some of Southern California's major metropolitan areas—until you travel their backroads.

The mountains visible in the Los Angeles Basin include the Santa Monica Mountains and the San Gabriel Mountains, both of which contain rocks 1.7 million years old, among the oldest on earth. The San Bernardino Mountains, east of the San Gabriel Mountains, begin just east of Interstate 15 and the Cajon Pass. These are the three "local" mountain ranges for Los Angeles, San Bernardino, and Riverside Counties. The San Emigdio Mountains, northwest of Los Angeles, rise just to the west of Interstate 5, while the Santa Inez Mountains and Topatopa Mountains lie east of the Coast Ranges, closer to Santa Barbara than Los Angeles.

While none of the Transverse Ranges see as much precipitation as the Sierra Nevada Range to the north, snow often dusts their peaks during the winter. The San Gabriels and San Bernardinos receive enough snow to attract thousands of downhill skiers each year. Mount San Gorgonio, in the San Bernardino Mountains, rises 11,502 feet above sea level, and Mount San Antonio in the San Gabriel Mountains, stands at 10,064 feet. In the San Emigdios, Mount Pinos, a favorite haunt of cross-country skiers, reaches 8,831 feet.

The south facing slopes of the Transverse Ranges, near the Los Angeles Basin, receive thirty to forty inches of rainfall annually. But this moisture evaporates with alacrity in California's sunny Mediterranean climate, in a condition known as the slope effect. These slopes are covered by chaparral, a type of vegetation that resists drought but is not resistant to fire. Humans have labored for over a century to suppress fires in the mountains of Southern California. Periodic and immense conflagrations have consumed the unnaturally thick stands of chaparral as well as the homes built in these often tinder-dry places. In contrast, the north-facing slopes, with just half the moisture of the southern slopes, contain moisture-loving coniferous forests that can reach from the upper slopes of the mountains almost to the floor of the desert.

Active earthquake faults separate all the Transverse Ranges. One day, in an unimaginably distant future, these mountains may shift direction as new convulsions shape the earth. Until that happens, roadway adventurers can explore these mountains over a variety of beautiful backroads.

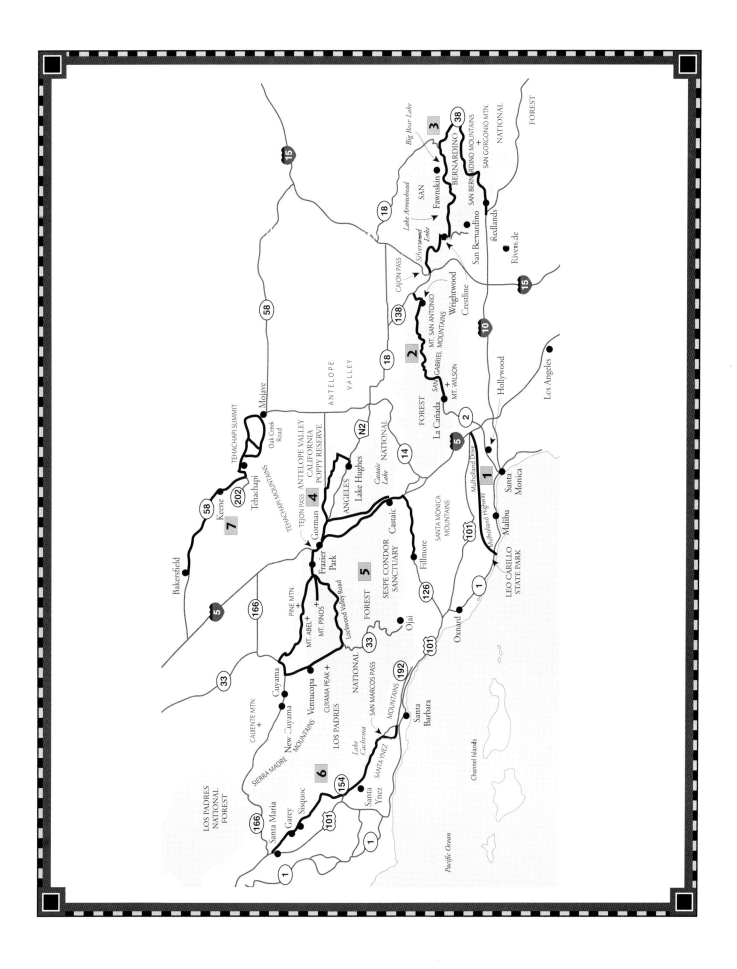

The entrance to the magnificent Malibu Hindu Temple beckons travelers to the Santa Monica Mountains.

The Old Place, a restaurant along Mulholland Highway, displays its menu on the side of an old mining cart.

The Santa Monica Mountains are reflected in a quiet pool at Malibu Creek State Park.

AN URBAN WILDERNESS
The Santa Monica Mountains

ROUTE 1

Access the east end of Mulholland Drive from Cahuenga Boulevard, in the Cahuenga Pass, between the Los Angeles Basin and the San Fernando Valley. Follow Mulholland Drive west through the Santa Monica Mountains; the roadway changes names to Mulholland Highway in Topanga Canyon. Continue following west, ending at the Pacific Coast Highway (California Highway 1).

"There it is. Take it."
—William Mulholland

The Santa Monica Mountains offer a striking counterpoint to the adjacent megalopolis that is Los Angeles. The Santa Monicas do not lack residential and commercial development; still, these mountains contain thousands of undeveloped acres that present a quiet refuge from the city. While development constantly threatens, more than one hundred fifty thousand acres are protected as part of the Santa Monica Mountain National Recreation Area (SMMNRA).

One road travels the length of the mountains from Griffith Park to the Pacific Ocean, a fifty-mile journey. That road is Mulholland Highway. The highway was named for William Mulholland, the controversial architect of the massive system of aqueducts bringing water to Los Angeles. Mulholland arrived in Los Angeles from his native Ireland in 1877 and went to work digging trenches for the Los Angeles City Water Company. He rose to become the self-educated superintendent and chief engineer of the city's water department, a post he held for more than forty years.

Completed in 1913 at a cost of about $24 million, Mulholland's 233-mile-long aqueduct carried water from the snowmelt on the east side of the Sierra Nevada. For Los Angeles, the aqueduct offered the potential for unlimited growth. As water first flowed into the city, Mulholland gave a five-word speech to commemorate the event: "There it is. Take it." Meanwhile, farmers in the once verdant Owens Valley, at the base of the mountains, watched their land dry out and Owens Lake turn into a bowl of dust.

Renamed Mulholland Drive in 1939, the eastern half of the highway is arguably the most scenic drive in Los Angeles. The enormous amount of residential development here has lessened but not ruined the roadway's wonders. Mulholland Drive offers unmatched views over downtown Los Angeles, Hollywood, the San Fernando Valley, and the San Gabriel Mountains. The highway also passes a number of reservoirs constructed by Mulholland for Los Angeles.

The Santa Monicas are not towering mountains; they reach, at their highest, a little above two thousand feet. But they have been in the making for thirty million years. Today, some of the ridge tops have been planed flat to accommodate upscale housing tracts. The mountain lions are mostly gone, but plentiful numbers of bobcats, coyotes, rattlesnakes, deer, raccoons, skunks, owls, and hawks still inhabit these mountains. Except for the hawks, these animals tend to put in appearances only after humans have retired for the evening.

Here and there along Mulholland Drive, the parklands of the SMMNRA preserve some open space. Franklin Canyon offers a pristine look at the mountains, and, despite its proximity to downtown Beverly Hills, the hiking trails here almost never become crowded.

But the highway really comes into its own as a backroad west of

Topanga Canyon Boulevard, where the rural and at times wild nature of Mulholland Highway asserts itself. The highest peaks in the Santa Monicas are here. Latigo, Kanan, Encinal, and Decker Canyons meet Mulholland Highway; each canyon features its own road leading down to the sea. Stunt Road reverses direction, traveling above the highway to offer spectacular views over the coastline to the south, as well as over the San Fernando Valley and the Transverse Ranges to the north.

The highway also passes along Malibu Creek State Park, which was once home to the back lot of 20th Century Fox studios. The 1968 classic *Planet of the Apes* was filmed here, as were the movie and television versions of *M*A*S*H*. Today the park contains a campground with a grand view of massive volcanic outcroppings. Miles of trails invite hikers and mountain bikers through chaparral-covered slopes and oak groves. Other wilderness parks with Hollywood connections include actor Peter Strauss's ranch and Paramount Ranch, both donated to the state.

The movie sets in the mountains are gone, but the striking Malibu Hindu Temple sits just across the road from Malibu Creek State Park, off Las Virgenes Road. Farther west, the Rock Store's café and '50s-style gas pumps attract hordes of motorcycle riders every Sunday.

Both Mulholland Highway and the Santa Monicas reach the Pacific Ocean and the Pacific Coast Highway (California Highway 1), as well as Leo Carrillo State Park. The park is a favorite of outdoor enthusiasts, including surfers, kayakers, scuba divers, and hikers, all of whom enjoy the broad beach, tide pools, coastal caves and reefs, a large campground, and the trails that travel into the upper reaches of the Santa Monicas.

The park was named for the actor best known for his role as the sidekick Pancho on the popular 1950s television show *The Cisco Kid*. Carrillo, a descendent of a prominent California family and a dedicated conservationist, played an important role in securing the land for the park. Given Carrillo's connection to the entertainment industry, it is appropriate that the park frequently serves as a backdrop for movies and television shows. No harm is done by lingering at the park until the end of the day, when the ocean waves seem illuminated as if within, and the setting sun baths the Santa Monica Mountains in a golden light.

From the park, the Pacific Coast Highway travels along the base of the mountains, where they touch the sea. Frenetic Los Angeles lies less than an hour away.

STAIRWAY TO THE HEAVENS
The San Gabriel Mountains

Over a century ago, William Brewer, first assistant to the Geological Survey of California, labored a few hours to climb the San Gabriel Mountains just north of Los Angeles. Today, travelers can make a similar journey by car in a matter of minutes. Several backroads lead into the mountains, but the Angeles Crest Highway, California Highway 2, the main road through

William Mulholland rose from immigrant ditch digger to lead the Los Angeles Department of Water and Power for more than four decades. He marshaled the labor of five thousand men for five years, to create the system of aqueducts that bring water to the city of Los Angeles. He also built a series of reservoirs that dot the Santa Monica Mountains. (Courtesy of the Los Angeles Department of Water and Power)

ROUTE 2

From La Cañada, take California Highway 2 (the Angeles Crest Highway) east into the mountains. Follow it to Wrightwood, then take Lone Pine Canyon Road south out of town, ending at the intersection with California Highway 138.

Fresh snow covers Mount Baldy, viewed from the Angeles Crest Highway.

The Clyde Ranch gas station, along Lone Pine Canyon Road, hasn't pumped gas since the early 1940s.

The East Fork Road crosses the east fork of the San Gabriel River.

the San Gabriel Mountains, offers the most bang for the buck. It travels sixty-five miles between the foothill city of La Cañada, on the west end of the mountains, and California Highway 138 in the Mojave Desert, on the east end.

Much of the San Gabriel Mountains reside within the Angeles National Forest. Initially known as the "San Gabriel Timberland Reserve," then the "San Gabriel National Forest," the Angeles National Forest contains miles of hiking and mountain biking trails, six downhill ski areas, superb trout fishing in its rivers and creeks, and thick forests of oak and pine. Alpine peaks rise more than ten thousand feet above sea level, providing inspirational views over the southern California landscape, including the San Gabriel Valley and Los Angeles Basin to the south and the Mojave Desert to the north. Bighorn sheep still roam the high country; black bears and even mountain lions occasionally wander into the densely populated foothills.

Switzer's Picnic Area, one of many stopping points, lies about ten miles north of La Cañada. Willows, maples, and oaks shade the picnic tables. A two-mile walk leads to fifty-five-foot-tall Switzer's Fall.

The turnoff to Mount Wilson, at Red Box junction, lies about fourteen miles from La Cañada. The prominent mountain owes its name to Benjamin Wilson, a fur trapper and trader who became a southern California land baron and, in 1851, mayor of Los Angeles. He also built a trail up Mount Wilson and briefly logged the mountain's timber.

The Mount Wilson Observatory, founded in 1904 by George Ellery Hale, has proved a far more durable and important enterprise. Astronomers continue to use Hale's one-hundred-inch telescope, the largest in the world at the time it was built. Hale's observations helped prove that our galaxy does not revolve around the sun and that our universe contains billions of galaxies beyond our own Milky Way.

Charlton Flats, back on the Angeles Crest Highway, is at five thousand feet in elevation. Here the vegetation changes from chaparral to pine. Charlton Flats boasts a comfortable picnic area underneath a canopy of ponderosa and sugar pines. A 1.5-mile trail leads to the top of Vetter Mountain, where weekend visitors can enjoy the view from the fire lookout during the fire season.

The Chilao campground and its visitor center lie about three miles east of Charlton Flats. Hiking and mountain biking trails start near the campground. Birders sometimes spot red-breasted sapsuckers, white-breasted nuthatches, and blue-gray gnatcatchers.

Southern California boasts more than a dozen ski areas, including six in the San Gabriel Mountains. Skiing became popular here after a ski-jumping craze caught the public's fancy in the 1930s. The Mount Waterman ski area, less than ninety minutes from downtown Los Angeles, put Southern California's first chair lift into operation in 1942. The non-profit Buckhorn Ski/Snowboard Club, just up the road from Mount Waterman, operates its own small ski area and its members are justifiably proud of their rustic, 1950s-era ski lodge.

Astronomer George E. Hale oversaw construction of the Mount Wilson Observatory, in the San Gabriel Mountains. Here Hale works on his invention, the spectroheliograph, a special camera designed to photograph the sun. (Courtesy of the Carnegie Institution)

Continuing on, the Angeles Crest Highway features more trailheads and vistas, including good views of Mount San Antonio. Its gray summit rises above the tree line, lending Mount San Antonio the unofficial name Mount Baldy.

The highway finally reaches Wrightwood. Tucked into the head of forested Swarthout Canyon, Wrightwood is a pleasantly unpretentious resort community. It was named for ranchers Sumner and Kate Wright, who settled in the area early in the twentieth century.

Angeles Crest Highway continues east along Highway 2 from Wrightwood, traveling down a side canyon to meet Highway 138. Long ago, the road from Wrightwood led not east but south, down Swarthout Canyon. That route, along Lone Pine Canyon Road, can still be followed out of Wrightwood. It passes the historic Clyde Ranch, which dates to the 1870s. A few buildings remain, including an old service station that last pumped gas in the 1940s.

A few miles past the ranch, the road reaches Highway 138, at the eastern end of the San Gabriel Mountains. Travelers can return the way they came or explore the Mojave Desert by driving north on Highway 138. To the south, where Highway 138 meets Interstate 15, the backroads of the adjacent San Bernardino Mountains lure visitors into more of the high country of Southern California.

UP TO THE RIM OF THE WORLD
The San Bernardino Mountains

Half the fun of exploring the massive San Bernardino Mountains lies in the journey to reach them. Of the various paved routes into the mountains, the most scenic is California Highway 38, which begins just north of the city of Redlands.

Long ago, Redlands, sitting on a mesa at the base of the San Bernardino Mountains, functioned as the center of the vibrant Southern California citrus industry. Although some of the citrus groves remain, urban sprawl has surrounded the city named for its rich red soil. Redlands is part of the "Inland Empire," which also includes the cities of San Bernardino and Riverside. Yet despite the development and proximity of a major freeway, Redlands retains the look and feel of small-town America.

The Inland Empire colonies were developed as planned communities in the 1870s. By 1890, Redlands, with its scenic backdrop of the San Bernardino Mountains, had attracted a contingent of wealthy citizens, who had fled the harsher climates of the East and Midwest. Many of these newcomers became town benefactors who left lasting monuments. The A. K. Smiley Public Library receives national attention for its beautiful Moorish architecture. The Lincoln Memorial Shrine, the only museum dedicated to Abraham Lincoln west of the Mississippi River, is adjacent to the library. To see the library and shrine, take the Orange Avenue exit off Interstate 10.

ROUTE 3

Exit Interstate 10 at Redlands and take California Highway 38 east into the San Bernardino Mountains. Follow to California Highway 18 (also called Rim of the World Highway or Drive), heading north and west. Reach California Highway 138 at Crestline and follow it west to Interstate 15.

RIGHT:
Daffodils line the highway at the community of Running Springs, along the Rim of the World Highway.

BOTTOM LEFT:
The beautiful A. K. Smiley Public Library, dedicated in 1898, was designed by Redlands architect T. R. Griffith. The architecture shows off its Spanish and Moorish influences.

BOTTOM RIGHT:
Big Bear Valley is home to innumerable bears, most of them carved. This one stands guard in the front yard of a home. Big Bear Lake is in the background.

The Kimberly Crest House is the crowning achievement of Victorian architecture in Redlands. Most of the mansions were built with money earned from the citrus industry.

Redlands is also home to more than three hundred Victorian-era "Marmalade Mansions," built by citrus industry magnates. Several of these homes open their doors to the public, among them the Kimberly Crest House and Gardens. Built on more than six acres in 1897, the three-story mansion, and its attendant gardens and citrus groves, were designed to look like a French chateau. Take the Ford Avenue exit off Interstate 10 and follow the signs to Prospect and Highland Avenues.

From Redlands, Highway 38 travels toward California Highway 18, the Rim of the World Highway (also known as the Rim of the World Drive), which leads into the scenic heart and soul of the San Bernardino Mountains. Highway 38 is not the fastest road up the San Bernardinos, but it has the least amount of twists and turns and relatively little traffic.

Highway 38 passes several campgrounds and trailheads. One of the more popular areas is Barton Flats, where visitors set up tents in the summer and put on cross-country skies in the winter. Side roads off Highway 38 lead to the San Gorgonio Wilderness. Mount San Gorgonio, at 11,449 feet above sea level, is the highest peak in California south of the Sierra Nevada. Also known as Old Grayback, its alpine summit rises high above the tree line. A dozen trails lead around the peak or to its summit.

The Rim of the World Highway travels the length of the San Bernardino Mountains. Stretches of the highway pass through pine forests and offer occasional views over the Inland Empire. Much of the route runs through or near the region's resorts, including popular Big Bear Lake. The lake sits in beautiful Big Bear Valley, seven thousand feet above sea level. Except for the little community of Fawnskin, which offers a modicum of services, the north side of the lake remains relatively undeveloped. The south side of the lake has been heavily commercialized.

Pioneer Benjamin Wilson named the valley in 1845, after he and his men traveled through the area and killed eleven grizzly bears in one day. Hunters extirpated the grizzly—California's official state animal—early in the twentieth century, though the valley still has lots of bears, hundreds even. They are carved in blocks of wood, fronting area homes and businesses.

Big Bear Valley also has a close connection with Redlands. The dam that holds back the waters of the lake was constructed so that the Redlands citrus growers could irrigate their orchards. When it is plentiful, water is still sometimes released to help irrigate the land around Redlands. Today, the lake is managed primarily as a recreational asset for Big Bear Valley.

Holcomb Valley lies a few miles north of Big Bear and marks the site of a short-lived gold rush in 1860. The valley's pine forests, creeks, and meadows can be explored on several good dirt roads. During the Civil War, Belleville was home to many Confederate sympathizers. Today, virtually nothing remains of the town. The gold is long gone, too, but the valley is rich with hiking and mountain biking trails. Visitors who want

"No outing in California is more cherished than this. On the one side lies the desert, on the other the land of the orange, the olive and the rose."
—Fredrick Tabor Cooper,
Rider's California, a Guidebook for Travelers, 1925

to spend the night can stay at the Holcomb Valley Campground.

Winter often buries Holcomb Valley and much of the mountains under several feet of snow. That's just fine for cross-country skiers, who glide down the relatively flat roads and trails in the Holcomb Valley. Downhill skiers and snowboarders, who glide down the slopes of several ski areas in and near Big Bear, also welcome the snow, which in some years can begin falling in October and continue as late as May.

Man-made Lake Arrowhead, west of Big Bear, is home to the swankest resort in the mountains. Built as an exclusive enclave for the wealthy, the town and its lakeshore sport many luxury homes.

The Rim of the World Highway reaches Highway 138 at Crestline, once a logging town, now a rustic resort community where cabins and homes cover the surrounding slopes. Highway 18 plunges down the south slopes of the mountains to reach the city of San Bernardino. But Highway 138 remains in the mountains for a while, continuing generally westward.

Highway 138 passes undeveloped Silverwood Lake, where patient visitors sometimes spot wildlife. Past the lake, the highway descends into high desert landscape, leaving the Rim of the World for good, and soon reaches Interstate 15 in the Cajon Pass, which marks the western end of the San Gabriel Mountains.

GOING FOR THE GOLD
The La Liebre Mountains and the Poppy Reserve

When the rains come at the right time and in the right amount, the hillsides, mountains, and deserts of California bloom with wildflowers. The backroads around the La Liebre Mountains north of Los Angeles are no exception. The color peaks anytime from mid March through May, when southern California's wildflowers are in full bloom.

The La Liebre Mountains ("liebre" means "jackrabbit" in Spanish) rise east of Interstate 5. The route around the mountains begins and ends in the Santa Clarita Valley, at the base of Castaic Dam, on the Ridge Route. Interstate 5 zooms north past the dam and travels up the mountains. But the Ridge Route, the first road built over the La Liebres, serves as the backroad into the mountains. With 647 curves along its thirty-six miles, the Ridge Route ensures a more relaxed drive into the Antelope Valley and over Tejon Pass.

The old highway was originally called the Tejon Route. ("Tejon" is the Spanish word for "badger.") It opened for traffic in 1915 as the overdue replacement for an old stagecoach line to the east that linked Los Angeles with the San Joaquin Valley. The start of the Ridge Route used to be over chaparral-covered slopes; the original landscape has been largely obliterated by a modern housing development. But past the homes, the La Liebre Mountains come fully into view. Ridges and mountaintops seem to stretch forever to the east, protected from commercial development and housing tracts within the boundaries of the Angeles National Forest.

ROUTE 4

From Interstate 5 at Castaic, take the Lake Hughes Road exit east to the Ridge Route. Follow the Ridge Route thirty-six miles north through the La Liebre Mountains to California Highway 38. Here, you have two options. The first option is to head west on Highway 138, turn north on Gorman Post Road, and head north on Interstate 5 to Tejon Pass. The second option is to head east on Highway 138 to the Antelope Valley California Poppy Reserve. From there turn south on Munz Ranch Road, then turn west on County Road N2 (Elizabeth Lake Road) and follow it to Lake Hughes Road.

A well-graded dirt road leads through the Antelope Valley California State Poppy Reserve.

The Rock Inn has long been a fixture in the La Liebre Mountains.

Colorful lupines and goldfields decorate the hillsides along Gorman Post Road.

The waters of the Castaic Lake State Recreation Area become visible, too, as the Ridge Route climbs high enough to allow a view over the top of the 425-foot-tall Castaic Dam. Boaters, swimmers, and anglers use the fore bay below the dam, as well as the lake behind it.

This is chaparral country, where plants grow densely together but rarely reach more than ten feet in height. The one native tree found in any abundance along the Ridge Route is the scrub oak, a sort of dwarf tree. In spring, bright red Indian paintbrush and purple lupine grow along the road. The vegetation has almost overgrown the remaining traces of the commercial enterprises once found along the highway. Only a few foundations, rock walls, and concrete steps remain.

At the northern end of the La Liebre Mountains, the Ridge Route offers a terrific look into the Antelope Valley and the adjacent Tehachapi Mountains. The road then drops out of the mountains into the western end of the Antelope Valley to reach Highway 138. Wildflower and history enthusiasts should take Highway 138 west to Gorman Post Road, part of the original Ridge Route. Gorman Post Road heads north a few miles along the base of the Tehachapi Mountains. Devoid of much vegetation most of the year, the Tehachapis are covered with colorful poppies and lupines during the spring. In good years, it looks as if Mother Nature has poured buckets of purple and gold paint over the landscape.

Interstate 5, which offers a quick return toward Castaic and Los Angeles or a rapid descent into the San Joaquin Valley, is just to the north, along Gorman Post Road. So is Tejon Pass, 4,411 feet in elevation. According to legend, Tiburcio Vasquez, one of old California's most infamous bandits, used the canyons around Tejon Pass as a hideout. Hard facts about Vasquez himself are open to conjecture. Was he captured in Los Angeles, near Pasadena, or in the Tejon Pass? We do know his last word, uttered just before he was hanged on March 19, 1875: "Pronto."

Those interested in more wildflowers and history need to retrace their way to Highway 138 and follow it east. This high-desert landscape in rural Antelope Valley lies between the Tehachapi and La Liebre Mountains. The vast and largely open terrain stretches for miles; in the spring, the valley is covered with poppies, the state flower of California.

The Antelope Valley California Poppy Reserve resides in the Antelope Buttes, about thirty miles east of the community of Gorman and just south of Highway 138, at the base of the La Liebre Mountains. The reserve hosts the most consistent displays of poppies in California. Visitors can drive over dirt roads flanked with wildflowers, walk along seven miles of hiking trails, or explore the visitor center, which displays a collection of watercolor paintings by the noted and self-taught wildflower artist Jane Pinheiro.

"The outlaw and several of his companions were off their guard near the Tejon Paso."
—Harris Newmark, *Sixty Years in Southern California, 1853–1913*

A 1920s postcard illustrates the meandering course of the Ridge Route between the community of Castaic, to the south, and the Antelope Valley, to the north. The old road offers sweeping views across several of the Transverse Ranges.

Munz Ranch Road travels from the edge of the poppy reserve into the La Liebre Mountains to reach Elizabeth Lake Road (County Road N2). The forest service maintains a few parking areas along the lake where visitors can fish or picnic.

Lake Hughes, a small fishing lake, and the community that bears the same name, lie about four miles to the west. The unpretentiously rustic Hughes Lake Shore Park opened to the public in 1985; guests can pitch a tent or park their RV, rent a rowboat, fish for catfish, or go for a swim. At the west end of the lake, Painted Turtle Camp, a summer camp for children with life-threatening illnesses, opened in 2003 and was funded by actor Paul Newman.

The Rock Inn has been a Lake Hughes landmark since 1929. A fire gutted the previous structure, an inn and general store built by local resident Joel Hurd Sr. His second attempt, which has stood the test of time, employed steel instead of wood and foot-and-a-half-thick walls made of concrete and covered with river rock. Today, the Rock Inn's restaurant, bar, and patio tables make it a favorite Sunday destination for motorcyclists.

Lake Hughes Road, at the west end of the lake, travels down a narrow canyon and back into Angeles National Forest. The canyon is filled with cottonwoods much of the way. Cottonwood Campground offers a cool, shaded respite about four miles down the canyon. The road continues for another twenty scenic miles before climbing out of the canyon and up a final ridge, where there are impressive views of the surrounding mountains and, just below, Castaic Lake.

WINGED VICTORY
Condor Country

The California condor is the largest flying animal in North America. Its wingspan can stretch to ten feet, and its weight can reach twenty-five pounds. Captains Meriwether Lewis and William Clark, during their epic exploration of the Louisiana Purchase, documented the condor's bald head, as well as the white triangular patch under its wings that, besides its size, distinguishes it from other vultures. Clark also correctly surmised that condors scavenge carrion, noting that his expedition saw condors dining on dead beached whales and fish.

Less than a century later, in the early 1900s, only about six hundred condors remained on the continent. By 1980, condors were almost extinct. Victims of shooting, pesticide poisoning, and human encroachment on their wild homelands, only about fifteen survived. The condors, capable of flying at heights of fifteen hundred feet and traveling more than 150 miles in a day, made their last stand in a tiny enclave in the Transverse Ranges, not far from Mount Pinos.

Thanks to a massive state and federal program that first captured, then bred, and now releases the giant birds back into the wild, condors

ROUTE 5

From Interstate 5, take the Frazier Park exit and drive west on Frazier Mountain Park Road, which will become Cuddy Valley Road past the junction with Lockwood Valley Road. Turn right onto Mount Pinos Road and follow it west to its termination below the summit of Mount Pinos.

To reach Lockwood Valley, retrace your route down Mount Pinos Road and turn right onto Lockwood Valley Road. Follow Lockwood Valley Road south to California Highway 33. Turn right on Highway 33 and follow it north as it merges with California Highway 166. Turn right onto Cerro Noroeste Road and follow it east to Mil Portrero Highway, which in turn becomes Cuddy Valley Road and leads back to Frazier Park.

To reach the Sespe Condor Sanctuary from Frazier Park, follow Interstate 5 south to California Highway 126. Turn right onto Highway 126 and follow it west to Fillmore, then turn right onto "A" Street going north. This becomes Goodenough Road; follow it to the Sespe Condor Sanctuary.

Snow dusts a portion of the Cuyama Badlands. The sandstone badlands, formed in fresh water rather than salt water, are unusual in California.

A condor soars above the Topatopa Mountains, north of Fillmore.

This close-up view of a California condor shows off the bird's distinctive bald head. (Courtesy of U.S. Department of Fish and Wildlife)

can again fly the skies over Mount Pinos. Several condors have been released at the Hopper Mountain National Wildlife Refuge to the south. Other condors have been released near Big Sur and at Pinnacles National Monument in California, as well as near the Grand Canyon in Arizona, and in Baja California, Mexico. Well over one hundred condors now exist in captivity and in the wild.

While spotting a condor is a rare treat, condor country offers much more to explore, even without glimpsing the mighty birds. Their territory covers an enormous area, part rural, part wilderness, loosely bounded by Interstate 5 to the east, California Highway 33 to the west, California Highway 126 to the south, and California Highway 166 to the north.

One backroad—the Mount Pinos Road—travels most of the way up the mountain, through a thick forest of ponderosa, Jeffrey, and sugar pines. The road can most easily be reached by traveling west from Interstate 5 and the little community of Frazier Park. The road stops below the summit of Mount Pinos, in a parking lot next to a small campground and picnic area.

On evenings from summer through fall when the moon is dark, this parking lot becomes one of the best stargazing sites in southern California. It's filled with a collection of astronomers who are happy to offer strangers a look through their telescopes. On my first nighttime visit to Mount Pinos, I remembered to bring warm clothing, but I didn't dim my car's headlights as I drove into the parking lot, much to the annoyance of the stargazers. With the bright stars overhead, the company of the astronomers and their telescopes, and Gustav Mahler's symphony "The Planets" playing on someone's portable speakers, the night became magical.

The end of the paved road is the jumping off point for an easy 1.7-mile walk or mountain bike ride along a broad dirt road to the top of Mount Pinos. The trail, a favorite destination for cross-country skiers during the winter and spring, leads across open meadows and past a stand of rare limber pines, which can reach several hundred years in age and grow to an average height of about forty feet. The summit itself provides a perfect perch from which to scan the skies over the Transverse Ranges for condors.

The Spanish gave Mount Pinos its official name (which means Pine Mountain). At 8,831 feet above sea level, Mount Pinos stands as the tallest mountain in the Transverse Ranges west of Interstate 5. The Chumash people call the mountain Iwinhimu, loosely translated as "Place of Mystery," and it is the Chumash center of the universe. For the Chumash, the most sacred animal is the condor. Much of the mountain is a protected part of the Chumash National Wilderness, off limits to any sort of commercial development or mechanized travel.

The easiest way to reach Mount Pinos is from Interstate 5, via the little community of Frazier Park. This route is also the quickest to picturesque Lockwood Valley, dotted with small ranches, and lacking commer-

"This bird fly's very clumsily, nor do I know whether it ever seizes it's prey alive, but am induced to believe it does not."
—William Clark, *Journal of Lewis and Clark*, February 16, 1806

cial services for about twenty-five miles. Turn on Lockwood Valley Road to twist and turn through the Cuyama Badlands, sharply eroded layers of sandstone that formed under water millions of years ago.

Camp Schiedeck is a few miles short of the junction of Lockwood Valley Road and California Highway 33. The "camp," situated at the base of the badlands along trout-stocked Reyes Creek, was an old-fashioned resort, first operated by German immigrant Martin Schiedeck in the late 1890s. A few dozen cabins, some rustic, some upscale, remain on the property, along with the old saloon and restaurant. A small private campground, complete with showers, sits next to the saloon. The more primitive National Forest Reyes Campground is just up the creek.

The resort town of Ojai lies south of the Lockwood Valley Road on Highway 33. To the north, Highway 33 travels past the pastures and orchards of the Cuyama Valley, which is the pistachio growing capitol of the United States. At the little community of Ventucopa, visitors can purchase flavored pistachios, including chili-lemon and onion-garlic varieties.

Past Ventucopa, Highway 33 reaches Highway 166. The tiny communities of Cuyama and New Cuyama are just to the west, where the Buckhorn Café features a fine view of the Caliente Mountains out its front window and a collection of western memorabilia inside.

Continuing north on Highway 166 (which merges for a while with Highway 33) soon leads to Cerro Noroeste Road, which travels around the northern flanks of Mount Pinos. This open country offers sweeping views over the San Rafael and Sierra Madre Mountains. It's a good place to look for condors.

Cerro Noroeste Road turns a corner, and the open land gives way to a forest of pinyon pines. The road follows a deep and steep canyon created by the movements along the San Andreas earthquake fault. When it reaches a forested pass, Cerro Noroeste Road bends right to climb to the top of Mount Able, where there is a small forest service campground. From here, a trail crosses a long ridge that traverses east to reach Mount Pinos.

Where Cerro Noroeste Road turns right to climb Mount Able, it meets Mil Portrero Highway, which continues around Mount Pinos. A few miles away is the Pine Mountain Club, where some two thousand residents live in homes tucked into the woods. Surrounded by national forest land, the Pine Mountain Club includes tennis courts and a golf course. Breakfast patrons at the club's Condor Café can order ham and cheese on a bun, listed on a menu as a "condor sandwich."

After a few steep grades, the Mil Potrero Highway becomes Cuddy Valley Road, which travels through rural Cuddy Valley before returning to Frazier Park and Interstate 5.

The pleasant town of Fillmore, at the base of the rugged Topatopa Mountains, is on the southern border of condor country. "A" Street travels a few miles north from Highway 126 toward the mountains. Once past orange and avocado groves, "A" Street becomes Goodenough Road, angles

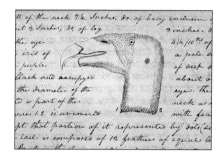

A Lewis and Clark journal entry for February 16, 1805, includes a written description and a drawing of a California condor. The travelers encountered the giant birds on the coast of what is now the state of Washington. By the late 1980s, there were approximately fifteen condors in the wild, all in California. (Courtesy of the American Philosophical Society)

The Sisquoc Church, constructed in 1875, marks the entrance to Foxen Canyon and the Santa Barbara County backcountry.

An eighteenth-century wine press graces the grounds of the Foxen Winery.

The sun sets behind an oak tree, high on the flanks of Figueroa Mountain.

sharply uphill, and narrows to one lane. As the road climbs, there are stupendous views of the backcountry.

After seven miles, the road dead ends on the edge of the Sespe Condor Sanctuary, another condor observation point. But condors are apt to be spotted anywhere above Goodenough Road, particularly over the eastern ridges along the first half of the road. These crests border the Hopper Mountain National Wildlife Refuge, which is closed to the public. The condors like to roost in this sanctuary. On days when the sun-warmed air begins to rise, so do the condors, who are once again free to soar anywhere they wish over condor country and beyond.

THE BRITISH ARE COMING!
The Santa Inez Mountains

ROUTE 6

From U.S. Highway 101 at Santa Maria, exit onto Betteravia Road and follow it east. Betteravia Road becomes Foxen Canyon Road near Garey. From Foxen Canyon Road, turn south onto California Highway 154 (San Marcos Pass Highway). Exit at Stagecoach Road and follow it to San Marcos Pass. A quarter mile past the pass, turn right onto Kenivan Road. Regain Highway 154 South, then turn right onto Old San Marcos Pass Road. Follow the latter to its junction with California Highway 192 (Foothill Road), near downtown Santa Barbara.

Several scenic backroads offer varied yet connected passages deep into the interior regions of the Santa Inez Mountains. These roads north of Santa Barbara travel through sparsely populated valleys and climb into the mountains to reward travelers with superb views of the Santa Barbara backcountry.

I prefer to begin from this trip from the north, exiting U.S. Highway 101 at Betteravia Road, near the city of Santa Maria. The route first travels through open farmlands. After a few miles, near the tiny farming community of Garey, Betteravia Road becomes Foxen Canyon Road. An equally small community, Sisquoc ("meeting place" in the language of the Chumash), lies a few miles south. For the next twenty miles, the road travels past more farmlands, vineyards, and thirteen wineries.

Foxen Canyon is named for William Benjamin Foxen, captain of an English merchant ship. Foxen came ashore in Santa Barbara around 1827. He met and fell in love with a local woman, Eduarda de Carmen Osuna, whom he married in 1831. The Mexican government later granted Foxen property north of Santa Barbara, which he named Rancho Tinaquaic (Chumash for "big creek").

During the 1846 Bear Flag Revolt, when California gained independence from Mexico, Foxen guided the forces of General John C. Frémont over San Marcos Pass—avoiding, according to legend, a possible ambush in the more accessible Gaviota Pass. Despite serving the American cause, Foxen would say in his later years that life had been better under the rule of Spain and Mexico. Today, a direct descendent of Foxen owns the rustic Foxen Vineyard winery, where the original barn built by Eduarda and William still stands.

The San Ramon Chapel, also called the Sisquoc Church, still stands, too. Constructed with redwood boards, the church was built in 1875 by another Englishman, Fredrick Wickenden. He married one of Foxen's daughters. The little cemetery behind the church is filled with the headstones of many pioneers, including Eduarda and William.

Foxen Canyon Road reaches a junction with San Marcos Pass Highway (California Highway 154). Figueroa Mountain Road lies just south of the junction. It travels up the mountain on a single lane, first past farmlands and vineyards and then through oak and pine forests. As the road travels through Los Padres National Forest, it offers eye-popping overviews of the Santa Inez Valley, the surrounding mountains, and the Pacific Ocean far to the west. The drive up and down Figueroa Mountain can be made in a few hours, but campgrounds and hiking and biking trails tempt visitors to stay longer.

Once off the mountain, Highway 154 continues south toward San Marcos Pass and past massive Cachuma Lake, which offers boating facilities, hiking trails, and an enormous campground. Exiting Highway 154 at Stagecoach Road leads under the Cold Stream Arc Bridge. The bridge, a single seven-hundred-foot span arching four hundred feet above the canyon floor, opened in 1963 as part of Highway 154, bypassing Stagecoach Road.

Beyond the bridge, Stagecoach Road arrives at the rustic Cold Springs Tavern, which originally served as the home of the Chinese laborers who built a turnpike over San Marcos Pass in 1868. After the road over the pass was completed, the home became a tavern and stagecoach stop. In 1910, the first cars traveled over the pass and put the stagecoach line out of business. Today, the tavern still has several original buildings and is a favorite weekend destination for those who enjoy live music and barbequed tri-tip.

San Marcos Pass, at 2,225 feet above sea level, is named for Father Marcos Amestoy, who once led the Santa Barbara Mission. The city of Santa Barbara, lying at the bottom of the far side of the pass, includes a whimsical melding of Spanish Mission Revival and Moorish architecture.

There are two wonderful backroads past the top of the pass. Watch for Kenivan Road on the right side of the highway, about a quarter-mile from the top of the pass. This beautiful but all-too-brief one-lane road runs past Kenivan Creek, through a narrow canyon thick with oaks and sycamores and several rustic homes.

After regaining Highway 154, look for Old San Marcos Pass Road, just south of Kenivan Road. This road roughly follows the old stagecoach route from Santa Barbara. This isn't a route for anyone afraid of heights. It has many steep switchbacks, including two hairpin turns with 270-degree curves, 5 mph speed limit signs, and jaw-dropping views over Santa Barbara, the Pacific Ocean, and the Channel Islands. The road passes by some splendid homes and avocado groves before leveling out and entering a residential neighborhood. Old San Marcos Pass Road drops out of the Santa Inez Mountains to end at California Highway 192 (also called Foothill Road here), not far from the Santa Barbara Mission and downtown Santa Barbara.

> *"It seemed strange to see people living so absolutely isolated—cut off from all the interests that affect the race, both in the past and present."*
> —Mary Cone, *Two Years in California*, 1876

LEFT:

The front end of a freight train rolls over its back end while passing through the Tehachapi Loop.

ABOVE:

The Keene Deli is a throwback to post–World War II diners.

ROUTE 7

From Bakersfield, take California Highway 58 east, then exit at the Woodford-Tehachapi Road. Go south three miles, then turn left onto the unsigned dirt road at Loop Ranch to view the Tehachapi Loop. Back on Woodford-Tehachapi Road, go south to California Highway 202 and the town of Tehachapi. Follow Highway 202 east to California Highway 58 South, then take the Tehachapi-Monolith exit.

To return to Tehachapi, turn onto Tehachapi Boulevard, turn right onto Tehachapi-Willow Springs Road, then continue to Cameron Canyon Road, which leads back to Highway 58.

To continue down the mountain into the Mojave Desert, skip Cameron Canyon Road and take Oak Creek Road to the town of Mojave and California Highway 14.

In 1853, the U.S. government sent Army Lieutenant R. S. Williamson on a mission to find a railroad route into California. Williamson and his scout, Alexander Godey, made their way over a pass in the Tehachapi Mountains, already long in use by American Indians, Spanish explorers, and miners.

Williamson named the pass and the mountains around it after a creek that local tribes called Tah-ee-chay-pah. The meaning of that name translates as "land of many acorns and good waters." Today, that route is closely followed by busy, multi-lane California Highway 58, which travels over the Tehachapi Pass between the San Joaquin Valley and the Mojave Desert. But the backroads that loosely parallel Highway 58 are far more inviting.

Exit Highway 58 at the little community of Keene and follow the Woodford-Tehachapi Road. The road passes the gravesite of labor leader Cesar Chavez at the headquarters of the United Farm Workers Union.

Three miles from the Keene exit, take a left on the unsigned dirt road at Loop Ranch to view an engineering marvel that draws railroad enthusiasts from around the world: the Tehachapi Loop. The Southern Pacific Railroad created this feat following Lieutenant Williamson's recommendation to put tracks over Tehachapi Pass. The problem was that the steep rise in elevation taxed the then-current level of technology. The solution is a unique structure for the train tracks. Heading southeast out of Keene, the tracks reach an entry tunnel. They then make a complete counterclockwise loop, 3,799 feet in length, which passes over the top of the entry tunnel. Because some freight trains extend more than a mile, a locomotive will, depending on the direction it's going, circle over or under the last cars of its own train. The loop was built by Chinese workmen who had once labored in the gold fields.

The railroad route from Bakersfield to the Tehachapi summit was dedicated on July 10, 1876. Today, more than forty freight trains a day travel over the Tehachapi Loop. While the tracks over the pass lie next to the Highway 58, the famed loop is only visible from the backroads. A mile past Loop Ranch, a National Historic Landmark and a National Historic Civil Engineering Landmark commemorate the construction of the Tehachapi Loop and the rail line. From the landmarks, visitors enjoy an excellent view of the loop and the Tehachapi Mountains.

Woodford-Tehachapi Road winds through the rugged and mostly undeveloped Tehachapi Mountains and climbs high above Highway 58, which is occasionally visible. The road reaches California Highway 202 and the town of Tehachapi in the Tehachapi Valley. The town was founded in 1876, when workers completed the rail line. Downtown Tehachapi, including Tehachapi Boulevard, runs right along the railroad line. The locals enjoy their morning coffee at the Mountain Crossing Coffee Shop, which features a scale model of the Tehachapi Loop in its lobby.

The signature event in the history of Tehachapi occurred on July 21, 1952, when an earthquake destroyed almost the entire downtown district. The temblor remains one of the most powerful in California's history, reaching 7.7 on the Richter Scale. A historic warehouse, one of the few buildings to survive the quake, sits about a dozen feet from the tracks. Renovated in 1996, the building now goes by the name Apple Shed, and includes a restaurant, bakery, fudge factory, and gift shop. The Tehachapi Museum, on Green Street, displays numerous Old West and American Indian artifacts.

"From the Indians we learned that their name for the creek was Tah-ee-chay-pah."
—Lieutenant R. S. Williamson, Railroad Survey Report, 1853

East of town, more than five thousand wind turbines cover the slopes of the Tehachapi Mountains. Strong northwest winds allow the futuristic-looking machines to generate enough electricity to power more than half a million homes. The turbines sprouted in the 1980s, in the wake of the prior decade's energy crises, making California the first state to develop large-scale wind farms.

Travelers can see the wind farms from Highway 58. For more leisurely views, take the Tehachapi-Monolith exit. The Monolith cement plant, built in the early 1900s and still in operation, provided cement for the Los Angeles aqueduct project. To return to Tehachapi, follow Tehachapi Boulevard one mile past the cement plant and turn right onto Tehachapi-Willow Springs Road, then continue to Cameron Canyon Road, which leads back to Highway 58. Wind turbines are visible all along the way.

If Lieutenant Williamson and Alexander Godey were to be plucked from the mists of time and returned to the Tehachapi Mountains today, they would no doubt be astounded to see the massive amount of rail and automobile traffic traveling up and over Tehachapi Pass. They would marvel at the technologically advanced windmills and probably enjoy a drive in a "horseless carriage" along busy Highway 58.

By taking Oak Creek Road rather than Cameron Canyon Road, aficionados of backroads can enjoy an alternate route down the eastern side of the mountains. This quiet road travels over hillsides dotted with oaks before reaching the desert at California Highway 14 and the little town of Mojave. It is a route more in keeping with the way the American Indians, the Spanish, the gold miners, and Williamson and Godey saw the landscape so long ago.

PART II

THE CENTRAL COAST

FACING PAGE:

The surf washes over ancient rocks at Montana de Oro.

ABOVE:

A smart billy goat seeks refuge from inclement weather in a doghouse along Santa Rosa Creek Road, near the town of Cambria.

Southern California's once pristine coastal regions have seen more commercial and residential development than their counterparts to the north. Real estate development is particularly rampant from Los Angeles County south to the Mexican border.

But the coastline and adjacent mountain landscape change north of Los Angeles County. From Santa Barbara all the way north to Santa Cruz, the tides of development have slowed or halted.

There is another kind of development taking place in the Coast Ranges. From the Oregon border in the north to the Transverse Ranges in the south, the Coast Ranges began to rise from the sea millions of years ago. Forces generated below the surface of the earth ultimately lifted these mountains thousands of feet above sea level. Still geologically active today, these ranges occasionally produce powerful earthquakes that shake the Central Coast, and the central and southern mountains are still rising, about a millimeter a year.

A fair amount of rain lashes the Central Coast during winter. In winter and spring, the grasslands and pasturelands along the coast and on the lower slopes of the Coast Ranges turn a brilliant emerald green. In summer, dense and damp fog often rolls over the coast. Despite that moisture, from late spring through autumn the landscape changes from green to "California Gold."

The wilder reaches of the Central Coast give shelter to bobcats, coyotes, kit foxes, turkey vultures, and even condors. While you may not see all these animals, you're almost guaranteed to spot the sociable California sea otters and northern elephant seals. Once hunted to the brink of extinction, both species have made strong recoveries due to international protection. Otters roam the southern California coast from Monterey Bay to as far south as Pismo Beach, and elephant seals have formed new rookeries on the beaches and coves around San Simeon.

The Central Coast also has its landmarks. Morro Rock rises almost six hundred feet above Morro Bay, gigantic waves break over the rocks near the Piedras Blancas lighthouse, and Hearst Castle sits high on a ridge top. But some things along the coast are hidden. A lost city lies buried in the sand just west of the little town of Guadalupe.

U.S. Highway 101 can make speedy work of the Central Coast. But why rush through a landscape that took millions years to create when you have so many backroads from which to choose?

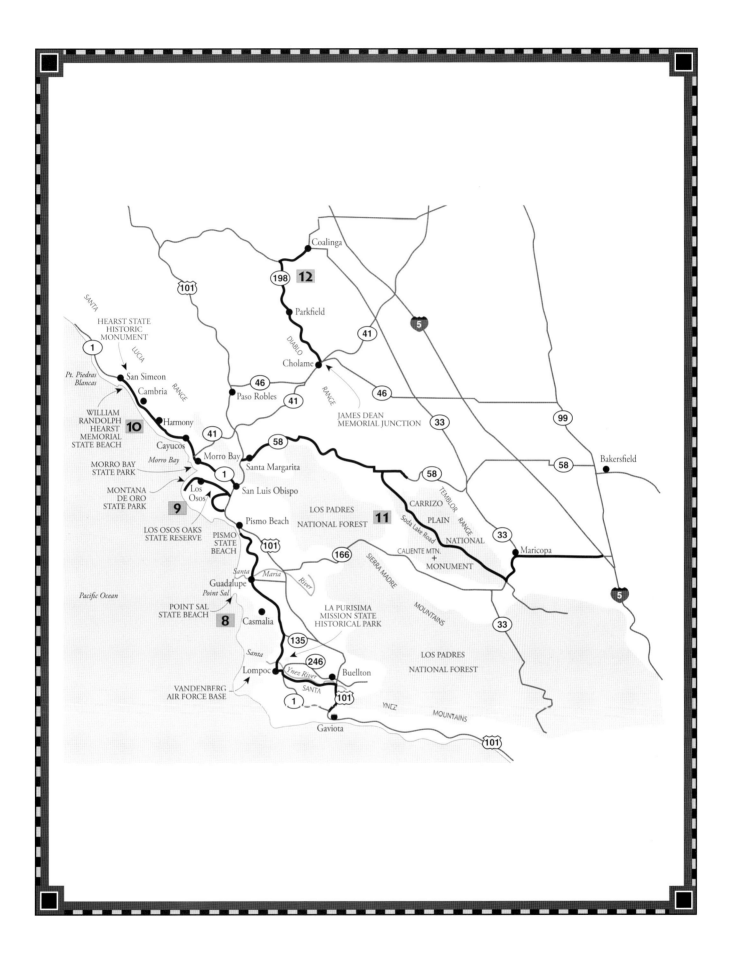

Coalinga

198 **12**

Parkfield

101

5

41

SANTA

HEARST STATE
HISTORIC
MONUMENT

LUCIA

Cholame

1

41

JAMES DEAN
MEMORIAL JUNCTION

*Pt. Piedras
Blancas*

San Simeon

Cambria

46

46

DIABLO

99

RANGE

Paso Robles

41

33

WILLIAM
RANDOLPH
HEARST
MEMORIAL
STATE BEACH

10

Harmony

RANGE

58

Bakersfield

Cayucos

41

58

58

MORRO BAY
STATE PARK

Morro Bay

Morro Bay

1

Santa Margarita

TEMBLOR

MONTANA
DE ORO
STATE PARK

9

Los
Osos

San Luis Obispo

LOS PADRES
NATIONAL FOREST

11

CARRIZO

RANGE

PLAIN

LOS OSOS OAKS
STATE RESERVE

Pismo Beach

Soda Lake Road

33

Maricopa

PISMO
STATE
BEACH

101

166

NATIONAL

SIERRA MADRE

CALIENTE MTN.
+
MONUMENT

Santa

Maria   *River*

5

Pacific Ocean

Guadalupe

Point Sal

POINT SAL
STATE BEACH

8

Casmalia

LA PURISIMA
MISSION STATE
HISTORICAL PARK

33

LOS PADRES
NATIONAL FOREST

MOUNTAINS

Santa

135

Lompoc

246

Buellton

Ynez River

VANDENBERG
AIR FORCE BASE

SANTA

1

101

YNEZ

MOUNTAINS

Gaviota

101

The Oceano Dunes lie south of Pismo Beach. They are part of the most extensive coastal sand dunes in southern California.

A great blue heron sits on a piling at dune-dammed Oso Flaco Lake.

Mist shrouds a farm along Highway 166, west of Guadalupe.

Exit U.S. Highway 101 at Buellton, about forty-five miles north of Santa Barbara, onto Santa Rosa Road and travel west. Turn right onto old California Highway 1 North. Turn right on Purisima Road to reach the La Purisima Mission. Leaving the mission, turn right onto Harris Grade Road. Go north to California Highway 135. Head west on Highway 135 to old Highway 1. Follow Highway 1 north into Guadalupe.

In Guadalupe, turn left onto West Main Street (also California Highway 166) and follow it to the ocean. Retrace Highway 166 back to Guadalupe, then take old Highway 1 north to Pismo Beach.

> *"I will destroy the city."*
> —Jeremiah 46:8,
> The King James Bible

North of Santa Barbara and Gaviota Pass, U.S. 101 turns away from the sea to wander the coastal mountains before returning to the coast at Pismo Beach. West of this inland wandering, a series of scenic backroads branch off the highway to explore the Central Coast.

California Highway 1 departs U.S. 101 on the far side of Gaviota Pass and travels toward Lompoc. But I prefer to exit farther north at the Santa Rosa Road, which travels west from Buellton through a scenic rural land-scape for about twenty-five miles. Mountains flank the left side of the road, farmlands and the Santa Inez River the right. The road ends at old Highway 1. Turn right and head north to Lompoc, a city known for its commercial flower fields and the many murals that decorate its commercial buildings. Continue north to reach La Purisima Mission, just east of Highway 1, on Purisima Road.

Perhaps the best restored of all the California missions, La Purisima sits on almost two thousand acres of otherwise undeveloped land. The eleventh of twenty-one missions built by the Spanish, La Purisima fell into ruin late in the nineteenth century. Ten of the original buildings were restored in the 1930s, including the chapel, the priests' and soldiers' quarters, the kitchen, and the women's dormitory. Visitors can wander through what is now La Purisima Mission State Historical Park, exploring rooms in the original mission buildings, as well as the five-acre garden. An outdoor corral contains burros, horses, goats, and longhorn cattle.

Occupying much of the coast west of Lompoc, Vandenberg Air Force Base launches rockets into space and usually stays off limits to the general public. One way to see it is on the daily run of Amtrak's Coast Starlight Express, which travels through the base over tracks paralleling the beach.

Just west of the mission, Harris Grade Road climbs steeply out of the Lompoc Valley, offering grand views over the Central Coast. On the far side of the grade, the road drops down to California Highway 135 in the Los Alamos Valley. U.S. 101 lies about ten miles to the east, while Highway 1 can be regained a few miles to the west.

Highway 1 travels through a beautifully rural landscape paralleling the east side of the Casmalia Hills, then crosses Brown Road, a few miles shy of the little town of Guadalupe. Brown Road climbs over Casmalia Hills and drops down to the remote Point Sal State Beach. The road periodically washes out and has been closed to auto traffic for several years. A hike or bike ride to the high point, about twelve hundred feet above sea level, offers an impressive view north and south over Point Sal and much of the Central Coast.

Unlike Point Sal, the Rancho Guadalupe Dunes are easily accessible by auto. These dunes, protected within the confines of a Santa Barbara County park, compose part of the largest dune complex found south of

San Francisco. The dunes lie just west of Guadalupe, where Highway 1 travels through the center of town. The old storefronts feature an amazing array of good Mexican restaurants.

The Dunes Visitor Center, at the north end of town, welcomes tourists in a restored 1910 Craftsman-style house, one of several beautiful homes in Guadalupe. The visitor center was probably built as a "catalog house," with the materials and architectural plans ordered from a catalog and delivered to Guadalupe by train.

To reach the dunes, turn left onto West Main Street (also California Highway 166) at the south end of Guadalupe. Follow the road a few miles to the parking lot at the edge of the ocean. To the south, a gigantic sand dune lies against the northern flank of the Casmalia Hills. The Santa Maria River estuary is just to the north of the parking lot. Lots of birds, including the endangered least tern, flock here.

These dunes harbor a mystery, too: a lost city of ancient Egypt may be buried here. When director Cecil B. De Mille filmed *The Ten Commandments* somewhere on this beach in 1923, he built what was at the time the largest movie set in the world and called his cinematic creation "The City

Does a city buried beneath the sand await resurrection? This photograph shows part of the massive set from The Ten Commandments, *filmed in 1923 by famed director Cecil B. DeMille on the Guadalupe Sand Dunes. Although DeMille reportedly ordered the set destroyed after filming was completed, some people believe much of the "city" remains intact underneath the dunes. (Courtesy of the Guadalupe-Nipomo Dunes Center)*

A replica of a spinning wheel helps recreate the authentic look of the beautifully restored La Purisima Mission, near the city of Lompoc.

FACING PAGE:
Monarch butterflies hang out in the late afternoon sun at Pismo Beach State Park.

The fertile farmlands along the central coast of California attracted thousands of migrants during the Great Depression. Photographer Dorothea Lange shot this image of Florence Owens Thompson and her children in 1936, in a migrants' camp near the community of Nipomo and U.S. Highway 101. Known as the "Migrant Mother," this may be the most famous Depression-era photograph. (Courtesy of the Library of Congress)

of the Pharaoh." To prevent other film companies from using his set, De Mille ordered it razed and buried beneath the dunes. Wood and plaster objects from the set are sometimes exposed after winter storms sweep the dunes. But despite efforts to uncover and restore the set, it remains, if it still exists, largely covered by the sands of time.

Beyond Guadalupe, Highway 1 travels through verdant farmland, parallels a more massive series of wild dunes, and passes the road to Oso Flaco Lake ("skinny bear" in Spanish). Oso Flaco owes its existence to the dunes, which block percolating ground water from reaching the sea, creating a chain of coastal lakes.

This stretch of coast is the one place in California where motor vehicles are allowed to drive on the beach. Cars can enter the beach at two entrances, located just south of the little resort town of Pismo Beach, and drivers can travel south almost as far as the Rancho Guadalupe Dunes.

The dunes east of the beach, except for one area open to dune buggies, prohibit motorized vehicles. A wilderness preserve protects these dunes all the way to where they end at Pismo Beach.

Where does the word "pismo" come from? Some believe it derives from the Chumash word "pismu" for the naturally occurring beach tar used to waterproof canoes. Others think it was the Chumash word for the famed pismo clam, prized for its size and flavor but nearly depleted in the 1980s by clammers and by a growing population of sea otters. A clamming ban has helped renew the clam population.

Pismo Beach is also home to monarch butterflies, who winter there from November through February. These monarchs, unlike their cousins east of the Rocky Mountains, do not migrate to Mexico. Instead, they travel up and down the California coast or east into the Sierra Nevada Range. The remarkable journey takes three or more generations of butterflies to finish their migratory round trip. Those that leave Pismo Beach will therefore not return. Instinctively, their descendants find the way back.

At Pismo Beach, more than two hundred thousand monarchs hang in giant clusters at night and during cool days. Whenever the temperature reaches 55 degrees, the monarchs flutter away from their clusters. As male and female monarchs look for mates, their orange and black wings stand out brilliantly against the blue skies and green trees. The clusters often form in a grove of eucalyptus trees in Pismo Beach State Park's North Beach campground. Parking for the butterfly grove is alongside Highway 1, and the campground lies just south of town. The butterflies also congregate in much smaller numbers at the state's Oceano Dunes campground, a little over a mile to the south, off Pier Avenue. Look for them in the Monterey pines, on the edge of the sand dunes.

THE LUCK OF THE IRISH
See Canyon to Montana de Oro

The coastal mountains meet the sea at Montana de Oro State Park. The pounding waves that carved great benches into the mountains over the course of countless eons continue to beat against the shore, and the mountains are still in flux. This mating of land and sea has helped to create one of California's most beautiful state parks.

Most visitors exit U.S. 101 at Los Osos Valley Road in the city of San Luis Obispo and travel fifteen miles west to the park.

A far more interesting but far less traveled route leaves U.S. 101 just south of San Luis Obispo. Exit on San Luis Bay Drive, then turn right onto beautiful See Canyon Road, which climbs the Irish Hills to bypass the urban clutter.

The narrow road winds through See Canyon for a few easy miles, up oak-forested hills and past several apple orchards whose owners count Central Coast residents as their steady customers. Past the farms, the road pitches abruptly upward and makes a series of switchbacks on the canyon's southern slopes. At the crest of a long ridge, the road tops out about twelve miles from the canyon's bottom. The oak trees thin out, and the road runs past several stately homes.

Looking south from the ridge top offers a view of more ridgelines and a view down into See Canyon. But the view north is more open, stretching across the Los Osos Valley to the Coast Ranges. Immediately across the valley, a line of twenty-million-year-old volcanic plugs, known as the Nine Sisters, marches from San Luis Obispo to the sea. The last of the plugs, Morro Rock, visible to the northwest, juts up from Morro Bay.

See Canyon Road becomes Perfumo Canyon Road on the north side of the ridge top. Another series of switchbacks drop down the flanks of the Irish Hills, which turn in spring as green as the Emerald Isle for which these mountains are named. At first, the road runs through open pastureland, then it reaches a forest of oaks and sycamores. The road's few short stretches of dirt wash out too often for the county to pave. Here and there, unpretentious, tree-shaded homes make an appearance.

Near the bottom of the mountain, the road passes through new housing developments before reaching Los Osos Valley Road. Turn left onto Los Osos Valley Road, heading toward the state park. With the Nine Sisters on the right and the Irish Hills on the left, the road travels west for ten miles, past commercial flowerbeds, ranches, and the ninety-acre Los Osos Oaks State Reserve. A one-mile hiking trail leads past ancient and enormous oaks covered in long, thick strands of Spanish moss. Strange dwarf oaks grow along the road, too, stunted by pockets of poor soil conditions.

Los Osos Valley Road runs through the center of the three-block Los Osos business district and continues past a residential area. Here the road

ROUTE 9

From U.S. Highway 101, north of Pismo Beach, exit onto San Luis Bay Drive, then turn right onto See Canyon Road and go up the Irish Hills. The road changes names to Perfumo Canyon Road on the north side of the ridge top.

Follow Perfumo Canyon Road down the other side of the Irish Hills and turn left onto Los Osos Valley Road. Go west through Los Osos. Past town, the road changes names to Pecho Valley Road. Follow it to Montana de Oro State Park and, beyond, to the ocean and Spooner's Cove.

> "A string of these buttes, more than twenty in number, some almost as sharp as a steeple, extend in a line northwest to the sea, about twenty miles distant, one standing in the sea, the Morro Rock, rising like a pyramid from the waters."
> —Henry Brewer, *Surveying California, 1860–1864*

FACING PAGE:
Wild mustard extends over the bluffs at Montana de Oro State Park.

ABOVE:
The tide pools at Montana de Oro are among California's finest. This sea anemone is one of many creatures found in the pools.

LEFT:
A sea star (also known as a starfish) lies in a tide pool at Montana de Oro. Sea stars are carnivorous and dine on hermit crabs, coral, clams, and even small fish.

Barns, stables, a creamery, and a house stood on the Spooner ranch, at what is now Montana de Oro State Park. A long chute led down the cliff from a warehouse to a boom that put cargo onto steamships docked in Spooner's Cove. (Courtesy of California State Parks)

changes names to Pecho Valley Road, which pivots south and climbs again into the Irish Hills.

The drive levels out a bit just past the entrance to Montana de Oro State Park. A few pullouts offer grand views over the southern edge of Morro Bay, including the great sand spit that forms the bay's outer edge. Morro Rock and the Coast Range mountains to the north also vie for attention.

Pecho Valley Road then travels past rows of eucalyptus trees, planted long ago in a futile attempt by Alexander Hazard to harvest them for lumber. Luckily for the trees, the fibrous wood proved a poor choice for houses and fence posts. Three miles beyond the park entrance, the road rounds a bend to reveal beautiful Spooner's Cove, named for pioneer rancher Alden Spooner. A rustic campground sits just out of sight near the mouth of the canyon that opens onto the cove.

The Bluff Trail leads down to the little beach at Corallina Cove. The tide pool in the cove is one of the best places in California to view sea anemones and hermit crabs; there might even be small fish and the occasional octopus. California harbor seals use the rocks beyond the cove as a favorite hauling out spot. I've rarely failed to spot a sea otter here. I've watched great blue herons land on a bluff and hunt rodents in the tall grass, and I've viewed long lines of pelicans swooping low over the breaking waves. Deer wander through the park's campground at dawn and dusk, and pesky raccoons sneak into the campground at night to steal food from unattended ice chests.

Montana de Oro comprises more than eight thousand acres and seven miles of coastline. Hiking and mountain biking trails climb the mountainous backcountry. The park keeps a horse camp tucked out of sight in a side canyon and opens some of its trails to horseback riders. Surfers test their skills and the waves at Hazard Reef.

Irene McAllister, the last private owner of the land that would become the park, named her ranch Montana de Oro ("Mountain of Gold" in

Spanish). When California purchased her land in 1965, the state wisely retained the ranch's name. Sometimes migrating gray whales spout off the coast, and fog half hides Morro Rock, while poppies bloom in profusion along the bluffs and up the flanks of the Irish Hills. At such times, the park truly becomes a mountain of gold.

THE PACIFIC COAST HIGHWAY
Morro Bay to San Simeon

The thirty-mile stretch of Highway 1 from Morro Bay to San Simeon is beautiful throughout the year. But Highway 1 especially entices travelers from December through the middle of February. During this time, the monstrously fantastic elephant seals make their appearance along the beaches at San Simeon, and the hills below famous Hearst Castle turn emerald green with winter's rainfall.

Picturesque Morro Bay and Morro Rock lie about thirteen miles west of busy U.S. 101 and the charming Central Coast city of San Luis Obispo. The bay and the rock received their name in 1542 from Spanish explorer Juan Rodriguez Cabrillo. Historians debate whether Cabrillo named the rock for the word that means "crown shaped hill" in Spanish, or whether the rock reminded the Spanish captain of a Moor's turban. Regardless, Morro Rock has served as a landmark for sailors ever since and may well have served the same purpose for American Indians.

The Chumash people first inhabited the land around the bay, including the stupendous sand spit that reaches out to enclose the bay and its estuary. American pioneers founded the town of Morro Bay in the 1860s. Today, it is a pleasant community supported by tourism and a fishing fleet. A walkway called the Embarcadero runs along the waterfront. The boats dock along a series of piers jutting out from the Embarcadero, and tourists stroll in and out of the curio shops and restaurants.

Sea otters, once hunted nearly to extinction, now enjoy protection under federal law. Otters frequent the bay, where they dive in the shallow waters for shellfish. The bay and estuary also harbor shore and sea birds, including pelicans, great blue herons, and snowy egrets. Morro Bay State Park, at the south end of town, includes a beautiful campground ensconced in a grove of eucalyptus trees, an eighteen-hole golf course, and a natural history museum perched on a little hill with a commanding view of the bay.

Morro Rock rises six hundred feet above the bay from the northern end of town. For many years, the rock was mined for material to build the Morro Bay breakwater. In 1968, the state declared Morro Rock a historical landmark, and the quarrying ended forever. Today, the rock is a bird sanctuary for the endangered peregrine falcon. It stands not just as a beacon for sailors but also as a beacon for tourists.

A few miles north of Morro Bay, the little town of Cayucos sits on a narrow strip of land between the mountains and the sea. The name of the

ROUTE 10

From U.S. Highway 101 at San Luis Obispo, take California Highway 1 thirteen miles northwest to Morro Bay. Follow Highway 1 north along the coast to San Simeon.

"Miss Morgan, we are tired of camping out in the open at the ranch in San Simeon and I would like to build a little something."
—William Randolph Hearst to architect Julia Morgan

ABOVE:
Morro Rock, almost six hundred feet tall, dominates the scene at Morro Bay.

RIGHT:
Hearst Castle is visible in the distance, behind the old one-room schoolhouse at San Simeon. No longer in use, the schoolhouse is now part of the state parks system.

Portrait of an elephant seal family: the proud husband stands guard as wives relax, argue, and nurse their offspring.

An elephant seal relaxes at the end of the rainbow. Hunted almost to extinction, the elephant seals have made a remarkable comeback, exploding in numbers along a stretch of southern California's central coast, between the Piedras Blanca Lighthouse to the north and the little community of San Simeon to the south.

town is an Aleutian word for "kayak." The beach, the fishing pier, and the quaint center square look much as they did when Cayucos was a nineteenth-century whaling town. Colorful murals decorate the sides of several buildings and recount the historic beginning of the town. Step into the old-fashioned candy shop or the Old Cayucos Tavern ("The Saloon" if you want to sound like a local), and step back more than a century in time.

Past Cayucos, Highway 1 runs close to the coast for a few miles before turning inland. In late fall and winter, the road winds over the green foothills of the Coast Ranges. Highway 1 soon reaches the turnoff to Harmony, a community that encompasses just one short block. Once a center for dairies (called creameries a hundred years ago), Harmony now boasts a collection of shops, a restaurant, and the post office, all in one old creamery building. The glassblower occupies a smaller building, a winery sits atop the nearby hill, a few homes are scattered around "town," and the population hovers around twenty residents and a few horses.

How do you pronounce the name of the much larger town six miles up the coast? Visitors usually say "Camebria," while most locals say "Cammbria." However you pronounce it, Cambria will delight you with its equal measures of class and kitsch. Tucked into a small valley along Santa Rosa Creek and surrounded by a forest of Monterey pines, this resort town is replete with art galleries and upscale restaurants. It boasts a renowned bike shop and a toy soldier store, as well as Victorian and Tudor-style architecture. Camozzi's, the local saloon, is more than a century old (and looks it); here, Central Coast bands rock the locals on weekends. Moonstone Beach Drive at the town's north end runs along a dark sand beach, past restaurants, motels, bed and breakfasts, and a little park on top of the bluff.

Santa Rosa Creek Road leads east from Cambria's Main Street. This delightful backroad climbs high into the Santa Lucia Mountains, past farms and ranches settled by nineteenth-century pioneers. It's worth driving five miles up the canyon to stop at the Linn family's landmark farm store, made famous by its olallieberry pies.

A state campground and a collection of motels lie a few miles north of Cambria. The William Randolph Hearst Memorial Beach, a few more miles north, features a fishing pier and picnic tables. Sitting next to a frontage road paralleling the highway here, the nearby Sebastian general store dates to the time San Simeon was a whaling village. The store's interior, regrettably modernized, is less cluttered than it once was but still displays harpoons used by the whalers. A one-room schoolhouse sits unused next to the store.

Across the frontage road from the store, a few buildings look as if they are part of a Spanish mission. Built in the 1920s, they were used to store the art and construction materials for Hearst Castle.

The entrance to Hearst Castle State Historic Monument lies just across Highway 1 from the Memorial Beach. The castle sits on a ridge sixteen hundred feet above the sea. Built by newspaper magnate William Randolph

Architect Julia Morgan meets with newspaper magnate William Randolph Hearst during the construction of Hearst Castle. Morgan designed more than seven hundred buildings and opened the door for women to work as architects in the United States. (Courtesy of Marc Wanamaker/Bison Archives)

Hearst, the castle was designed by architect Julia Morgan. Construction on La Cuesta Encantata (The Enchanted Hills) began in 1922. The castle was never completed; work halted in 1947. Casa Grande, the main building, contains 165 rooms, including a movie theater, 38 bedrooms, and 41 fireplaces. The architectural style, known as Mediterranean Revival, competes for visitors' attention with Hearst's enormous and eclectic art collection.

Hearst used the castle grounds—450,000 acres in total—to create what was then the world's largest collection of animals. Ahead of its time, the zoo featured open enclosures for tigers, apes, bears, yaks, and zebras.

When Hearst died in 1951, his castle was donated to California, though the Hearst family still controls much of the land here. While the castle is unchanged, the zoo was disbanded, but a few zebras still wander the property, occasionally visible from the highway.

Beyond the castle, the hills retreat from the rugged coast. Pullouts on the ocean side of the highway give access to small beaches and coves, several of which serve as rookeries for northern elephant seals. About a mile south of the Piedras Blancas Lighthouse, a viewing area, complete with a large parking lot and a boardwalk, provides a safe place for visitors to watch the seals. At the height of the season, hundreds of seals pack the beach.

Humans believed the northern elephant seals became extinct in 1880. However, a few elephant seals, perhaps fewer than one hundred, continued to breed on Guadalupe Island, off the coast of Mexico. Discovered and granted international protection, the seals made a slow recovery over the next century and now number over 150,000.

For many years, the best place to view the seals was at the Año Nuevo state reserve, south of San Francisco. But that has changed with the arrival of the seals at San Simeon. The seals return here each November, after almost a year of wandering the seas. From fewer than two dozen seals in 1990, a few thousand now grace the beaches of San Simeon. Once on the beach, the seals fight, mate, sleep, and give birth to their adorable pups.

Elephant seals are enormous, odd creatures. Some weigh up to five thousand pounds. The pendulous noses of the harem-seeking males give the species its name, and they use them as super sound chambers to intimidate each other. Occasionally, these massive creatures do serious battle, but most of the time it's all a big bluff. The rookery fills with the sounds of bellowing males, squawking pups, and the gargling grunts of the females.

Completed in 1875, the Piedras Blancas Lighthouse is named for three stupendous white rocks just off the coast. The Bureau of Land Management offers sporadic tours. The lighthouse marks a fitting finish to this backroad ramble. The return to San Luis Obispo takes less than an hour. The landscape ahead makes a decided change, as Highway 1 climbs above the rugged Big Sur Coast into the Santa Lucia Mountains.

Dirt tracks snake their way into the center of the Carrizo Plain. The eroded hillsides in the distance are part of the Temblor Mountains, shaped by the convulsive forces of the San Andreas earthquake fault.

Sheep, some recently shorn, graze on the northern fringe of the Carrizo Plain.

Tidy tips burst into bloom at Carrizo Plain National Monument.

Soda Lake, often dry, reflects the Temblor Mountains during spring.

FIND THE LOST WORLD
Carrizo Plain National Monument

ROUTE 11

Take California Highway 166 west from Interstate 5. Continue about twenty-five miles west and turn right on Soda Lake Road. Go northwest to California Highway 58. Turn left on Highway 58 and go west to Santa Margarita, just east of U.S. Highway 101.

"On the rolling plains of the Carrisa the people have but little to do with lawyers and judges."
—*San Luis Obispo Tribune*, 1897

Abandoned houses, barns, silos, and farm machinery offer visual evidence that the Carrizo Plain is a tough place to survive. Summer sun bakes the soil, and cold winter winds howl with unimpeded fury. Even today, roads that travel over the plain are few and rough; most are unpaved and impassible after heavy rainfall. Only the western portion of Soda Lake Road, between California Highway 58 and California Highway 166, is paved. A long stretch of Soda Lake Road to the east is unpaved, although it is well graded.

To the north of the plain, now designated as a national monument, the twisted, crumpled hills offer proof of great forces that have raged beneath the earth's surface. The Carrizo Plain is one of the best places in California to view the great San Andreas earthquake fault that runs much of the length of the state.

The Carrizo Plain is least cruel from late January through April, when the temperatures can be mild. Hillside grasses shimmer with the color of emeralds, and when the wildflowers bloom, sometimes the plain becomes a sea of living color.

The Chumash people, who first inhabited this land, called the plain Ko'owshup, or "Earth-Water." They depended on the animals of the plain for food. When the Spanish arrived, the Chumash way of life came to an end. Grazing cattle displaced the wild animals, and the Chumash either drifted away or were absorbed into the mission system. To the Spanish, the plain was Llano Estero, "Salt Marsh Plain." To the Americans who came next, it became the Carrisa, a corruption of "carrizo," the local Spanish word for cane or tall grass. The plain is still the Carrisa to the locals, who live at the west end on private lands.

Whatever its name, the basin that makes up Carrizo Plain National Monument stretches forty-five miles long and ten miles wide, and sits between the Temblor and Caliente Mountains, east of San Luis Obispo and west of Bakersfield. President Bill Clinton granted Carrizo Plain national monument status in 2001 to ensure its preservation. It provides sanctuary for the land itself, which no longer faces scarping and bulldozing or draining and damming. The Carrizo Plain protects a number of endangered species, and preserves many of California's native plants, grasses, and wildflowers.

Not many people have heard of the Carrizo Plain, and few come to visit. Facilities in this remote monument consist of a visitor center, two primitive campgrounds, and a few portable toilets. Gas is available in the towns of Maricopa to the east and Santa Margarita to the west. With the nearest public phone fifteen miles north of the visitor center, spotty cell phone reception, and no fresh water, this site entices only the most adventurous backroad travelers. One day, I stopped my car just shy of a rattlesnake taking its afternoon sun on the asphalt a few miles east of the visitor center. I watched the rattler for almost an hour and shooed away approaching cars—all three of them—before the rattler finally slithered into the grass along the roadside.

Tule elk and pronghorn antelope have been reintroduced to the monument, and sandhill cranes spend time on the shores of Soda Lake, in the center of the plain. The largest alkali wetland in central and southern California, Soda Lake attracts thousands of migratory birds each winter. Runoff flows into the three-thousand-acre lake each winter; with no outlet, the water simply evaporates by summer, leaving a vast field of shimmering salts on a dry lakebed.

The lake exists because movements along the San Andreas and San Juan earthquake faults some thirty million years ago caused the land in between to subside. The plain became a lake, almost an inland sea, filled by runoff from the surrounding mountains. Today, the lake has shrunk significantly.

Long after Soda Lake had begun to dry out, the Yokuts and Chumash peoples lived on and around the plain for perhaps thousands of years. Little physical evidence of their time on the plain remains, except for bedrock mortars where they ground acorns and their rock paintings, called pictographs. Several pictographs can be seen at Painted Rock, a natural rock amphitheater located a few minutes' drive and walk from the visitor center.

EARTHQUAKE COUNTRY
Coalinga to Cholame

The powerful San Andreas earthquake fault runs through California in an almost straight line from Hollister in the north to Taft in the south. The center of that line passes through the little community of Parkfield, dubbed the "Earthquake Capital of the World."

The backroad to Parkfield begins in Coalinga. Ensconced in the well-named Pleasant Valley, the town lies a few miles west of the San Joaquin Valley, at the intersection of California Highways 33 and 198. The rugged foothills of the Coast Ranges' eastern flanks surround the historic community.

The Southern Pacific Railroad built "Coaling Station A" in the late 1800s to haul low-grade coal out of Pleasant Valley. When the station became a town, its name shortened to Coalinga. By 1890, the search was on for oil instead of coal, and Coalinga for a time turned into a boomtown.

As pleasant a place as Coalinga is, the town has suffered a seemingly Biblical series of natural scourges, including random invasions of crickets, grasshoppers, and even stink bugs. In 1913, a "black flood" roared

ROUTE 12

From the city of Coalinga, take California Highway 198 west approximately eleven miles and make a left turn onto the Parkfield Grade heading south. That road eventually changes names to Parkfield Coalinga Road. Continue south to Parkfield then go another seventeen miles south to the junction with California Highway 41. One mile east is James Dean Memorial Junction, at the Y intersection of California Highways 41 and 46.

Cows have the right-of-way on the south side of Parkfield Coalinga Road.

The rustic Parkfield Inn is a good place to wait for the next earthquake.

LEFT:

Whimsical mailboxes attest to the rural heritage of Coalinga.

BELOW:

A barn sits in the Cholame Valley beneath the Gabilan Mountains, not far from the community of Parkfield.

<blockquote>
"…This place is destined to become prominent in due time."
—letter about the community of Parkfield published in the San Luis Obispo Tribune, 1899
</blockquote>

into town after a cloudburst swept through the oil fields. Watery sludge damaged property and contaminated the town's well water. For almost six decades afterward, homes needed one faucet for drinking water, and one each for hot and cold wash water. In 1972, Coalinga was finally able to draw water from a canal in the San Joaquin Valley.

On May 2, 1983, at 4:42 P.M., disaster struck again. A powerful temblor injured more than two hundred people, destroyed over eight hundred homes, and leveled the town's business center. Ironically, some of these building had been constructed with bricks recycled from the great 1906 San Francisco earthquake.

The town rebuilt itself. Today, visitors probably know more about the annual Horned Toad Derby, held each Memorial Day weekend, than the earthquake that almost killed Coalinga.

Heading eleven miles west on Highway 198 into the Coast Range, the highway reaches a junction with the Parkfield Grade. This spectacular road, mostly dirt, travels south, rising high on the slopes of the mountains. The initial few miles pass over reasonably level terrain. But then the road begins a steep climb, offering wonderful views across steep slopes

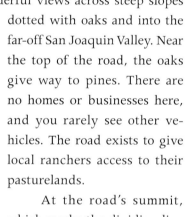

dotted with oaks and into the far-off San Joaquin Valley. Near the top of the road, the oaks give way to pines. There are no homes or businesses here, and you rarely see other vehicles. The road exists to give local ranchers access to their pasturelands.

At the road's summit, which marks the dividing line between Fresno and Monterey Counties, the Parkfield Grade changes names to Parkfield Coalinga Road, and the route down becomes rougher, although passable by passenger car. The little community of Parkfield lies at the bottom of the hill in the Cholame Valley. (Cholame is the Yokuts word for "beautiful place.") Grasslands and oaks dominate the now level landscape. Parkfield once bustled with homesteaders and

An earthquake struck the city of Coalinga on May 2, 1983, at 4:42 P.M. Downtown was destroyed, including the State Theater on Elm Street, pictured here. (Courtesy of the RC Baker Memorial Museum)

miners but today consists of just a motel, a restaurant, a gift shop, a few ranches, and about thirty-five inhabitants. Each year, Parkfield sponsors cattle drives, a rodeo, and a bluegrass festival.

The people of Parkfield call their home the "Earthquake Capital of the World" because temblors have struck the little community with an odd regularity. A moderate to major quake shook Parkfield about every twenty-two years, from at least as far back as 1857. Some believe the devastating quake that struck Coalinga in 1983 was meant for Parkfield.

Geologists wondered if the repeat quakes were unique to Parkfield. The United States Geological Survey and the State of California launched the "Parkfield Experiment" in 1986, setting up earthquake-monitoring equipment to understand what happens before, during, and after an earthquake. Residents expected the next temblor to strike Parkfield before 1993, but nothing happened. For whatever reason, Parkfield went untouched by temblors until 2004. On Tuesday, September 28 of that year, a magnitude 6.0 earthquake shook the little community for ten seconds. No one in Parkfield was injured, and property damage in the sparsely settled region was minor. But the information gathered will occupy geologists for years.

Seventeen miles to the south, the Parkfield Coalinga Road reaches California Highway 41. Less than a mile east, Highway 41 forms a Y intersection with California Highway 46 near a gap in the Temblor Mountains. On September 30, 1955, at six o'clock in the evening, a cultural earthquake struck California and the world when actor James Dean, age twenty-four, crashed his car at this highway junction.

Dean, who had just finished work on the last of his only three films, was on his way from Los Angeles to the Salinas Airport to race his silver Porsche. He had planned to tow his new sports car on a trailer behind his 1955 Ford station wagon. Instead, he took the wheel of the Porsche. Dean was barreling down Highway 46, just east of the highway junction and the little community of Cholame. At the same time, college student Donald Turnupseed was traveling in the opposite direction, on his way from San Luis Obispo to visit his parents in Tulare. Inexplicably, Turnupseed didn't see Dean coming, and he turned left off Highway 46 onto Highway 41, directly in Dean's path. The cars struck head-on. Turnupseed and a passenger in Dean's car survived, but the actor died.

The most fitting epitaph to Dean's life is perhaps summed up by the title of his final film: *Giant*. In death, Dean gained a cult status, which reverberates to this day like the aftershock of an earthquake. A steel and aluminum memorial sits next to the Jack Ranch Café in Cholame. The café is just east of where Dean was killed, which now officially bears the name James Dean Memorial Junction.

Known as the Black Flood, a sludge from a violent cloudburst in the winter of 1913 swept through nearby oil fields and inundated downtown Coalinga. (Courtesy of the RC Baker Memorial Museum)

PART III

THE SAN JOAQUIN VALLEY

FACING PAGE:

Abandoned structures stand throughout the San Joaquin Valley. This building, located near the community of Weedpatch, was used as a meeting hall of a migrants' camp during the Great Depression.

ABOVE:

Antlers lie on the ground at the Tule Elk State Reserve. The elk shed their antlers each winter and begin to grow new ones in the spring.

The geologic record of the San Joaquin Valley reaches back perhaps 140 million years, when the valley was an isolated arm of a western sea. Dinosaurs walked the earth and aquatic monsters swam the seas. Over the next several million years, the rising mountains of the Coast Ranges and Sierra Nevada washed muddy sediments onto the sea floor. The invading sediments slowly cut the inland sea off from its source and created the San Joaquin Valley.

The valley floor, which stretches fifty miles wide and about two hundred miles long, has rested a little above sea level for the past one and a half million years. But before it filled with mud, the sea thrived with fish, sharks, seals, water birds, and marine reptiles, including the mosasaur, the world's largest lizard. This voracious predator extended thirty feet long. After the sea dried up, mammoths, bison, giant ground sloths, and miniature horses roamed the valley floor.

The first humans who settled in the valley arrived some ten thousand years ago. They found deer, elk, antelope, and possibly bison and horses. When Spanish explorers arrived, they estimated about 85,000 American Indians inhabited the valley. Many villages held more than a thousand inhabitants. With the coming of the Spanish and then the Americans, the pace of life and culture changed rapidly. The American Indian communities were replaced by ranchos and then by towns that supplied the gold rush camps. But despite the changes, the San Joaquin Valley still offers a sense of wonder as well as awe-inspiring views that the first explorers enjoyed. The valley's backroads can connect travelers with both the land and the people.

The two major roads that span the length of the valley are Interstate 5, which runs along the valley's west side, and the older California Highway 99, on the east side. The more interesting corridors in the San Joaquin Valley have names such as Elk Hills Road, Sunset Road, and the Migrant Highway. These roads offer sweeping views of the valley's flat plain and the surrounding foothills and mountains. Straying from the main highways, the roads travel past some of the most productive fruit farms, vineyards, and cotton and oil fields in the United States.

BLACK GOLD
The Elk Hills

Early in the twentieth century, the west side of the San Joaquin Valley played an important role in the creation of California's oil industry. Where sheep once grazed the sparse grass and quail dashed across the old highways, the rural scenery had to share space with pipelines and oil wells.

Today, the area can be best be explored along several backroads that travel over and around the Elk Hills, which are really the top of great arch of folded rock—called a syncline by geologists—between the towns of Buttonwillow to the north and Taft to the south.

ROUTE 13

Take California Highway 166 west from Interstate 5 about twenty miles to the town of Maricopa. Take California Highway 33 north to the city of Taft. North of Taft, follow California Highway 119 to Elk Hills Road. Turn left on Elk Hills Road and go north. Near the town of Buttonwillow, stay straight to go on Buttonwillow Drive, take a right on Brite Road, take a right on Wasco Way, and take a left on Stockdale Highway. Follow the highway to the Tule Elk State Reserve.

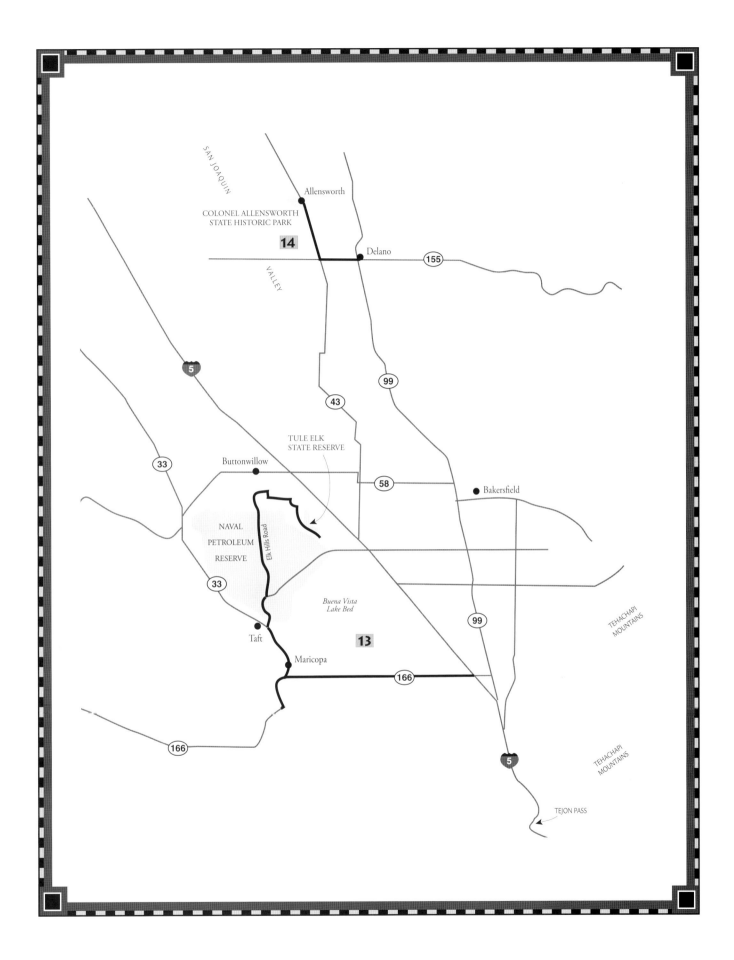

SAN JOAQUIN

VALLEY

Allensworth

COLONEL ALLENSWORTH
STATE HISTORIC PARK

14

Delano

155

5

99

43

TULE ELK
STATE RESERVE

33

Buttonwillow

58

Bakersfield

NAVAL

PETROLEUM

RESERVE

Elk Hills Road

33

Buena Vista
Lake Bed

13

99

TEHACHAPI
MOUNTAINS

Taft

Maricopa

166

166

5

TEHACHAPI
MOUNTAINS

TEJON PASS

Old pipelines travel between the wells and refineries in the historic Elk Hills, on the west side of the San Joaquin Valley.

Dawn light silhou-
ettes an oil well and
telephone and power
poles near the
community of
Tupman, at the base
of the Elk Hills.

LEFT:
A California quail
sits atop a pipeline
in the oilfields near
Maricopa. The bend
in the pipe helps
relieve uneven
pressure as oil is
forced through the
pipeline from the
fields to the refinery.

Workers try to revive the once massive flow of oil at the Lakeview Number 1 well with a new pipe. The blowout in 1910, the greatest gusher in California history, spewed more than nine million barrels of oil over the landscape, much of it unrecoverable. The new well failed to produce any significant amount of oil. (Courtesy of Bruce Petty)

The Elk Hills Road travels over the syncline, rising from either direction in a series of tight curves, to crest at more than fifteen hundred feet above sea level. Here, portions of the landscape have been scraped away to make room for an amazing assemblage of oil wells and pipelines used to extract and store the black gold.

The hills gained their name from the indigenous tule elk. Half a million elk once roamed the San Joaquin Valley, yet as gold and land rushes swept across California, their numbers dwindled. By the 1870s, a single herd of less than two dozen remained. A local rancher, Henry Miller, decided to protect the remaining animals on his extensive properties in the valley, thereby saving the elk from extinction. Today, the tule elk number about twenty-four hundred in locations throughout southern California, including the Tule Elk State Reserve at the base of the Elk Hills.

Like the preserve, much of the semi-desert land around the Elk Hills is treeless. In the spring, when wildflowers bloom, color splashes the hills. But displays of poppies and lupines are not the only inducements for exploring the Elk Hills. History also beckons.

In the early months of 1910, oil speculators had given up on the Lakeview No. 1 oil well, located at the base of the Elk Hills' east slopes, between the towns of Taft and Maricopa. Despite more than a year of drilling, the well had produced no oil. The order to shut down the well was made, but not before the driller, "Dry Hole Charlie" Woods, ordered the removal of a pipe that had stuck in the well hole. On March 15, 1910, as the drillers began to winch the pipe out, unsuspected pressure from the oil below blew the pipe into the top of the oil derrick, bringing forth the Lakeview gusher.

The plume of oil rose into the sky until it was visible for thirty miles. The flow soon reached ninety thousand barrels a day. Workers hurriedly built huge sandbag dams to keep "The Trout Stream" from reaching the Buena Vista Lake eight miles away. Their labor saved the lake, but less than half of the 9.4 million barrels of oil that washed over the landscape was recovered. The rest of the oil seeped into the ground or evaporated. All the oil gushed from a channel of sandstone only a few feet wide but a mile in length.

Thousands of roustabouts rushed to Taft to find work in the thirty-nine new oil companies launched within two weeks of the blowout. The boom also powered the growth of Taft, which began life as a tent city but grew quickly into a quintessential oil town. Little Maricopa, surrounded by oil fields, lies a few miles south on Highway 166. With just a single block of storefronts, the town retains a pioneer feel.

A year and a half after the gusher erupted, the flow of oil quit as suddenly as it began. Today the site of Lakeview No. 1 sits just off California Highway 33, on the old Taft-Maricopa Highway (now called Petroleum Club Road). All that remains amidst the barren landscape is a small crater surrounded by sand bags and a plaque commemorating "America's most spectacular blowout."

The giant Elk Hills Naval Petroleum Reserve, the tenth largest oil field in the continental United States, was established in 1911 to assure a ready supply of fuel for the ships of the U.S. Navy. The reserve figured in the infamous Teapot Dome Scandal, during the tainted presidency of Warren G. Harding. In 1921, Harding's Secretary of the Interior, Albert Fall, leased the Elk Hills reserve and the Teapot Dome reserve in Wyoming to private oil companies without asking for competitive bidding. Fall received $400,000 worth of kickbacks in cash, bonds, and livestock from the owners of the oil companies. The secretary's subsequent fall landed him a year in prison, making him the first Cabinet officer to go to jail for crimes committed while in office. Were he around today, Albert Fall might find it ironic that the U.S. government sold its interest in the Elk Hills Naval Petroleum Reserve in 1998 for $3.5 billion.

"I have concluded that the elk hills might have small scattered deposits of oil, but that they would not be important in an economic sense."
—Associated Oil Company geology report, 1910

FREEDOM ROADS
Delano to Allensworth

A few pleasant backroads connect Delano, the quintessential San Joaquin Valley town, with Allensworth, which was once the most atypical town in the valley. Different as they are, both towns have served as stopping points along the sometimes-arduous roads to freedom.

Delano, at the crossroads of the Garces Highway (California Highway 155) and California Highway 99, has long billed itself as "Table Grape Capital of the World." Viewed from Highway 99, Delano appears to be nothing more than a collection of gas stations and fast food restaurants. But just east of Highway 99, the town also offers residents and visitors a more traditional downtown of storefronts.

The Southern Pacific Railroad named the town in 1873 for Columbus Delano, a distant relative of future president Franklin Delano Roosevelt. Delano, who helped the railroad secure land in the San Joaquin Valley, is not remembered well by history. He served as Secretary of the Interior under the scandal-ridden presidency of Ulysses S. Grant and convinced Grant to veto a bill that would have protected American bison from extermination.

Like the rest of the San Joaquin Valley, Delano is an epicenter of migration. The town drew a large contingent of Yugoslavian immigrants, who

ROUTE 14

In Delano, exit California Highway 99 and travel west on California Highway 155 (Garces Highway). Turn right onto California Highway 43 for the five-mile drive to Allensworth.

This is the Colonel Allen Allensworth home in the state park bearing his name, in the heart of the San Joaquin Valley.

The schoolroom at Allensworth State Historical Park looks just as it did when students filled the chairs in 1915. The school closed in 1972.

Two cultures blend in Delano's La Michoacana Restaurant.

Grapes ripen by late September in the San Joaquin Valley. This vineyard is across the road from the United Farm Workers Union headquarters in Delano.

labored in the vineyards, as well as Mexican and Chinese railroad workers. In the mid-twentieth century, a large influx of Latinos began to settle in the San Joaquin Valley. One was Cesar Chavez, a Delano farm worker who would become a seminal figure of the American labor movement. Chavez knew the life of a farm worker in California was not an easy one. He and his family had labored in vineyards up and down the San Joaquin Valley, where Chavez attended thirty elementary schools. As an adult, Chavez settled in Delano, where he married Helen Febela; the two met while working together in Delano's vineyards. Chavez went on to found the National Farm Workers Association (NFWA). The union worked to win contracts with growers for better pay and benefits for members. In 1965, the NFWA joined what became known as the Delano Grape Strike. The farm workers prevailed after a five-year struggle, which included a worldwide boycott of California grapes.

Part of that struggle took place in the vineyards along the Garces Highway, west of Delano, where the farm workers have their Delano union headquarters. The union hall and a few other buildings stand on the north side of the old highway, on a plot of land known as Forty Acres. Here Chavez would hold historic meetings with labor leader Walter Reuther and attorney general Robert Kennedy. Beyond the union hall, the Garces Highway ends about five miles west of Delano, at an intersection with California Highway 43, an alternate north and south route through much of the San Joaquin Valley.

Labor leader Cesar Chavez is pictured in 1965, during a strike he helped organize in the San Joaquin Valley on behalf of migrant farm workers. (Courtesy of the Walter Reuther Library)

A right turn onto Highway 43 takes travelers north five miles, past more farmlands. A left turn onto Palmer Avenue heads over an embankment topped with a set of train tracks and leads directly into Allensworth State Historic Park.

The park is the site of the only California community founded, constructed, and governed by African Americans. The community was named for Colonel Allen Allensworth, a significant yet largely forgotten figure of American history. Allensworth, born in 1842 in Louisville, Kentucky, grew into adulthood as a slave. Although the education of slaves was illegal, Allensworth learned to read and write. He escaped slavery twice and was captured twice. He won freedom when he escaped a third time during the Civil War. He joined the Union Navy and by war's end was serving as a first class petty officer on a gunboat.

After Allensworth underwent a religious conversion, he successfully lobbied for a commission to serve as chaplain in the all-black 24th Army Infantry. He retired in 1906 as the highest-ranking chaplain and the highest-ranking African American in the U.S. Army.

Colonel Allen Allensworth was the founder of the San Joaquin Valley colony that bore his name. Pictured here in uniform, Allensworth retired as the highest-ranking black officer in the U.S. Army. (Courtesy of California State Parks)

Allensworth moved to Los Angeles where he met William Payne, a black educator. The two men decided to found an all-black colony and purchased almost nine hundred acres of fertile land in the San Joaquin Valley. Allensworth's name was the draw, and by 1910 the colony had built a town with an elementary school, drugstore, hotel, stores, churches, and restaurants.

In 1914, Colonel Allensworth was struck and killed by a motorcycle; some believe he was murdered. Without its leader, and facing prejudice from surrounding communities, the town began a slow fade, until the center of Allensworth was completely abandoned in 1966.

Allensworth and the town he founded weren't forgotten; Allensworth State Historical Park was created in 1976. A few of the original buildings still stand, including an impressive school building open for tours, and others have been painstakingly reconstructed. Visitors can stay in a small, tree-shaded campground attached to the park.

While Allensworth State Historical Park showcases what once was and speculates on what might have been, it would be wrong to call the community a failure. That's because Allensworth as a community still exists. County Road 84, at the entrance to the park, connects the old town site with a few hundred homes, many on small plots of land stretching over the flat countryside. County Road 24, off Highway 43, is an alternate route into the community. Most of the residents are Latinos, but a few African American residents trace their roots back to the earlier days of the twentieth century.

After visiting the park, it's easy enough to return to Highway 99 via the Garces Highway, or to make a more leisurely journey along Highway 43 through the orchards, vineyards, and pasturelands of the San Joaquin Valley.

PART IV

THE SIERRA NEVADA

FACING PAGE:

The rising sun illuminates the east face of Mount Whitney, viewed here from behind an intervening ridge near the end of Whitney Portal Road.

ABOVE:

A monarch butterfly with droopy antennae sleeps atop a coneflower on a cool morning in the Sierra Nevada.

The mountains of the Sierra Nevada range stretch more than four hundred miles along the eastern edge of the state. The climate ranges from semi-desert to alpine and varies in elevation from a few feet above sea level in the western foothills to more than fourteen thousand feet in the high country. The mountains are commonly called the Sierra Nevadas or the Sierras, but because the ridges are part of a single range, the correct form is the singular Sierra Nevada. These mountains make up the longest unbroken mountain range in the United States. (The Rocky Mountains are a collection of several ranges.)

Whatever it is called, this range basically consists of a single block of granite, called a batholith. This enormous block has been rising from beneath the surface of the earth for at least ten million years, and most of the uplift occurred in the last three million years. That makes these mountains relatively young. The famous jagged summits indicate that youth and help provide evidence that the Sierra Nevada was partly sculpted by glaciers, those rivers of ice that last swept over and around the peaks some twenty to sixty thousand years ago. A number of mostly small glaciers still exist on the east side of the Sierra Nevada, all of them either stationary or in retreat due to the recent warming of the earth's atmosphere.

Much of the uplift, essentially caused by the movements of the North American Plate against the Pacific Plate, occurred along the base of the east side of the mountains. This uplift tilted the batholith toward the west, dropping the western edge of the range beneath the sediments on the floor of the Great Central Valley. Because of the tilt, the east sides of the mountains are both steep and high.

Spanish explorers gave the mountain range its name. *Sierra* means "jagged range" or "saw," while *Nevada* means "snowed upon" or "frozen." Naturalist John Muir called the Sierra Nevada the "Range of Light." Like a bright beacon, it has attracted backpackers, climbers, mountain bikers, skiers, and snowboarders from around the world. Photographer Ansel Adams's name is almost synonymous with the Sierra Nevada, and the mountains have appeared in the backdrop of countless Western films.

In northern California, the Sierra Nevada harbors the blue waters of Lake Tahoe and the granite cliffs of Yosemite National Park. The range in the southern half of the state boasts the finest groves of giant sequoias and the highest peaks, including the tallest mountain in the contiguous forty-eight states, Mount Whitney, which stands 14,496 feet above sea level.

Much of the Sierra Nevada has been set aside as wilderness, open only to hikers and those on horseback. Even so, a plethora of backroads offer access to both the periphery and the interior of the Sierra Nevada.

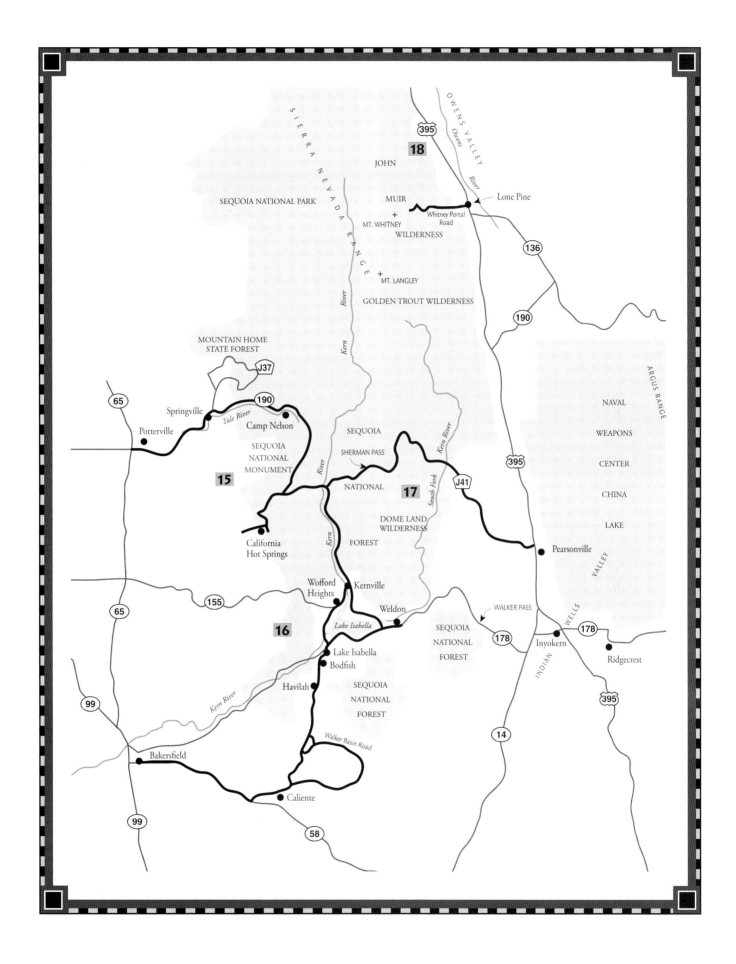

TOP LEFT:

A delicate tiger lily dangles at the edge of Quaking Aspen Meadow in Sequoia National Monument.

TOP RIGHT:

One of the prettiest Sierra wildflowers is the aptly named Shooting Star. These wildflowers love moisture and are usually the first to bloom in the mountain meadows.

RIGHT:

Dew-covered Bigalow Sneezeweed stands in Quaking Aspen Meadow. This beautiful flower is not a weed nor will it cause a sneeze.

A small pool of water is fed by a spring along the Trail of a Hundred Giants.

ROUTE 15

From Porterville, take Highway 190 east up into the Sierra Nevada range and Sequoia National Forest. Near the Quaking Aspen area, the highway becomes the Great Western Divide Highway (also County Road M107). Follow it south to Sequoia National Monument.

Where the Great Western Divide Highway ends, turn left onto County Road M50 to reach Lake Isabella. Or turn right onto County M50 to reach the resort community of California Hot Springs.

Sequoia National Monument is the less developed sibling of nearby Sequoia National Park. But what the monument lacks in gas stations, souvenir stands, and upscale lodging, it more than makes up for in scenery. Within the monument live massive sequoia trees, which by sheer bulk are the largest living things on earth. The site also boasts hiking and mountain-biking trails, spectacular granite spires that attract daring rock climbers, mountain meadows filled with wildflowers, and several lovely campgrounds.

A good place to begin a backroads journey into the monument is in Porterville, on the eastern edge of the San Joaquin Valley. Porterville, whose downtown exudes small-town charm, lies at the junction of California Highways 65 and 190, about fifty miles northeast of the city of Bakersfield.

From Porterville, the route to the monument heads east along Highway 190, past the Kaweah Reservoir and the turnoff to the Tule River Indian Reservation. The highway passes through Springville, a pioneer town settled, like Porterville, in the mid-nineteenth century. Emerald green in winter and spring, the rolling hillsides around Springville turn "California gold" the rest of the year.

Beyond Springville, Highway 190 enters the Sierra Nevada foothills and begins an arduous but worthwhile twenty-five–mile ascent onto the range's western slopes. After the highway enters Sequoia National Forest, it runs along the Middle Fork of the Tule River, where there are pullouts for anglers and swimmers. The road finally climbs above the river via a dizzying set of switchbacks. An old flume parallels the road for several miles, carrying water from the high country down to a power station and Springville. As the road gains significant elevation, the northwestern face of Slate Mountain, more than nine thousand feet in elevation, appears to the southeast.

The oaks and manzanita of the lower slopes gradually give way to incense cedars, sugar and ponderosa pines, and red and white fir. By the time the road reaches the tiny community of Camp Nelson, evergreens have almost completely taken over. Nine miles later, Highway 190 significantly straightens its course as it climbs to more than seven thousand feet above sea level. The highway turns south and reaches the Quaking Aspen area, where Highway 190 becomes the Great Western Divide Highway, also known as County Road M107, and reaches the border of Sequoia National Monument.

Quaking Aspen Campground is the prettiest place to pitch a tent in the Sierra Nevada. The meadow fills with wildflowers during the summer and offers easy skiing and snowshoeing during the winter. A hiking trail leads from the campground to the summit of nearby Slate Mountain. The trailhead to the Freeman Grove of giant sequoias lies just across the road, where a fifteen-minute downhill walk offers the first view of the giant trees. Beyond the Freeman Grove, a fourteen-mile drive along the North Road—half of it dirt—ends at the Golden Trout Pack Station.

Back on the Great Western Divide Highway, a turnoff leads to the trailhead for the Needles, which are a series of colossal granite spires that rise out of the forest floor, and the Kern River Canyon. To reach the trailhead, travelers turn left off the highway on a dirt road about a quarter mile beyond the campground. The Needles Fire Lookout perches spectacularly atop one of the spires. A short, level walk along the trail provides a good view of the lookout. Reaching the lookout itself demands a vigorous 2.5-mile walk. Enclosed on four sides with glass windows, the fire spotter opens the tiny, one-room home to all comers from nine o'clock in the morning until dusk.

The Ponderosa Lodge is on the highway about a mile beyond the turnoff to the lookout. The "Pondo" represents the only commercial enterprise in the area and sits adjacent to a neighborhood of homes, hidden by the forest, on private land surrounded by the monument. The locals gather at the Pondo's bar and restaurant, while the market caters to campers who forget to bring fry pans and marshmallows.

The turnoff to Dome Rock is about a mile past the Pondo on a dirt road. A short walk leads to the flat top of this massive granite outcropping, where visitors have a good view of the Needles; the tiny fire lookout is just visible on the leftmost spire. The view also looks over the enormous Kern River Canyon. In 2001, President Bill Clinton created Sequoia National Monument, which contains and protects much of the river canyon, as well as the groves along the Great Western Divide Highway.

Nine miles beyond Dome Rock, the highway reaches the "Trail of a Hundred Giants," where a self-guided half-mile trail wanders through the Redwood Grove of sequoias. The small Redwood Grove campground lies directly across the road.

The Great Western Divide Highway comes to an end about three miles past the Redwood campground. A left turn onto County Road M50 (also called Parker Pass Road) heads down the mountain through the Kern River Canyon to Lake Isabella. Or a right turn onto County M50 offers commanding views of the Sierra Nevada foothills and the San Joaquin Valley through breaks in the oak trees that predominate the landscape.

If you opt to turn right onto County M50, the road drops into a canyon and passes through the community of California Hot Springs. The old-fashioned resort there offers a good place for grungy travelers to grab a shower, soak in a Jacuzzi, swim laps, and order up an ice cream cone before returning to Highway 65, halfway between Porterville and Bakersfield.

"The proposed Roosevelt National Park will embrace…Mount Whitney, Tehipite Valley and the Kings and Kern Canyons."
—Fredrick Tabor Cooper,
Rider's California, a Guidebook for Travelers, 1925

Redwoods dwarf a human visitor to the Freeman Grove. The trees can reach more than two hundred feet in height, and some are more than two thousand years old.

This waterfall flows each spring and early summer along California Highway 190, on the route up to Sequoia National Monument.

CALIENTE TO KERNVILLE
The Road to Lake Isabella

ROUTE 16

From Bakersfield, take California Highway 58 east. Exit onto Caliente-Bodfish Road (also County Road 483) and go north to the town of Lake Isabella.

From Lake Isabella, follow California Highway 155 and Burlando Road north around the reservoir to Wofford Heights and Kernville.

To leave the mountains, retrace your route to Lake Isabella, then take California Highway 178 west back to Bakersfield or east to California Highway 14 North/South.

"Our Christmas was spent in a most unchristmaslike manner. Our camp was made on the slope of the mountain, at some Indian wells of good water."
—Edward M. Kern, journal entry, 1845

Lake Isabella and the Kern River Valley are popular destinations in the southern Sierra Nevada. The lake's dam, about forty miles east of Bakersfield, holds back the waters at the confluence of the North and South Forks of the Kern River to help prevent flooding as well as to provide power to the San Joaquin Valley. The area attracts outdoor enthusiasts who enjoy boating, whitewater rafting and kayaking, birding, fishing, car camping, hiking, and mountain biking.

Several roads lead to Lake Isabella. California Highway 178, which travels east from Bakersfield, is the most heavily traveled road. The upper portion of the highway is a four-lane freeway, but the lower section, which runs through the deep Kern River Canyon, is a two-lane and often congested highway.

A more interesting and certainly more leisurely route begins off California Highway 58, east of Bakersfield, over Caliente-Bodfish Road (County Road 483). This narrow road runs north from the community of Caliente, which once housed railroad workers, for about thirty miles, to reach the southern end of the Kern River Valley.

The section of old road just past the junction with Caliente Creek Road is as steep and winding as any in California. Much of the landscape includes oak forests and wild grasses. Once past the steep grade, the scenery alternates between secluded valleys and ridge tops as the road travels through cattle country.

A five-mile detour to the east along Walker Basin Road leads to the unusual Cowboy Memorial and Library. Opened in 1987 by cattle rancher and longtime cowboy Paul de Fonville and his wife, Virginia, the museum houses a vast collection of Western memorabilia in several walk-through trailers.

Back on Caliente-Bodfish Road heading north, travelers pass through the community of Havilah sitting in a pleasant canyon. The town took its name from a line in the Bible, Genesis 2:11: "land of Havilah, where there is gold." Once a thriving mining town, Havilah was for a time the Kern County seat. When the gold played out, the town faded into anonymity. Today, a few historic buildings still stand, interspersed between private residences and small ranches.

There are no fish in Bodfish, the little community north of Havilah and three miles south of Lake Isabella. But Bodfish, named for pioneer George H. Bodfish, does have its own ghost town. Really a museum, Silver City contains more than twenty historic buildings, including a jail, saloon, general store, and church. All the buildings were moved to Bodfish from their original locations in and around the Kern River Valley.

The first non–American Indians to explore the area were members of the Joseph Walker party. Walker was a larger-than-life figure from Tennessee who helped open up the fur trade in 1820 between the United

States and New Mexico, which was at that time a colony of Spain. In 1833, Walker and his men had crossed the Sierra Nevada from east to west. There were probably the first whites to view Yosemite Valley and the giant sequoias. On a subsequent expedition, Walker traveled up the Kern River Canyon into the Kern River Valley and made his way over the low pass east of the valley that is named after him.

The Kern River Valley was named in 1846 for cartographer Edward Kern. But the first visitors the valley, the Shoshone people, had arrived perhaps four thousand years earlier. They came from the desert lands to the east and called themselves the Tubatulabal people. By the time

Henry Stalvert, who worked in the gold mines around the town of Kernville, poses outside the Kern River Hotel early in the twentieth century. (Courtesy of the Kern Valley Museum)

Silver City is a collection of historic buildings moved to the community of Bodfish in the 1960s and 1970s. Silver City has reposed in near abandonment for so long that the ersatz ghost town has become a real ghost town.

Oaks dot the hillsides just south of Caliente-Bodfish Road.

LEFT:

The Cowboy Memorial, in the Walker Basin, was created by Paul and Virginia de Fonville. This offbeat, off-the-beaten-track museum, with its collection of cowboy memorabilia, is worth a visit.

BELOW:

The eastern edge of Lake Isabella, a magnet for boaters and anglers, sits beneath the Sierra Nevada range, here dusted with a late spring snowfall.

nineteenth-century explorers arrived, the Tubatulabal creation myth said that they had always lived in the Kern River Valley. The Kawaiisu were neighbors of the Tubatulabal. The descendants of both peoples as well as other tribes still live in and around the valley.

Miners traveled through the Kern River Valley after the 1848 discovery of gold in California. Gold was mined periodically in the valley over the next fourteen years. Mining camps grew into towns. As farms and ranches supplanted the gold fields, newcomers largely displaced the Tubatulabal people. In 1863, a U.S. Calvary detachment massacred thirty-five to forty of the remaining Tubatulablas in the valley.

When massive Lake Isabella Dam was completed in 1953, the resulting reservoir submerged much of the land and its history. The new lake flooded the town of Isabella, named in honor of the Spanish monarch who grubstaked Christopher Columbus' search for the New World; the town moved south, below the lake that took its name. The lake also submerged the pioneer town of Kernville, still quaint, which simply moved north.

The Kern River Valley Museum in Kernville is packed with exhibits and memorabilia about the history of the valley. South of Kernville, in the community of Wofford Heights, the American Indians in the valley have opened a cultural center, Nuui Cunni ("Our House"). Open to the public, the center tells the story of the past and promotes American Indian history and culture in the present. It is also a meeting place for tribal members from all over the valley.

The quickest return to the San Joaquin Valley is via Highway 178 to the west. Those headed to Los Angeles can choose a different route by following Highway 178 east through the valley, along the route Joseph Walker took. Fifteen miles east of Kernville, and not far from the eastern end of Lake Isabella, the National Audubon Society and the Nature Conservancy have established the Kern River Preserve near Weldon, a small community on the South Fork of the Kern River. The preserve, open every day from dawn to dusk, encompasses more than one thousand acres and the largest riparian lowland forest in California. Hummingbirds and turkey vultures migrate to the preserve each year, and hundreds of species of birds and plants live here year round.

Beyond the preserve, Highway 178 passes through the little ranching communities of Onyx and Canebrake. The mountains begin to close in on the road as it swings through a series of curves and climbs almost twenty-six hundred feet through a canyon, to reach Walker Pass. The view from that pass encompasses an enormous stretch of the Mojave Desert to the east. But a look back to the west, down the narrow canyon, reveals not a trace of the wonders to be found in Kern River Valley.

THE LAST ROAD
Across the Kern Plateau

The beautiful Kern Plateau lies near the southern end of the Sierra Nevada. While the peaks are not as high as those to the north around Mount Whitney, the Kern Plateau counts evergreen forests, mountain meadows, a river, strange rock domes, and beautiful views of the high country among its charms.

Old logging and ranching roads were linked in the late 1960s to create one route that crossed the entire Kern Plateau. When the Sherman Pass Road, Kennedy Meadows Road, and Nine Mile Canyon Road (County Road J41) were joined, they also created the last road to be paved across the Sierra Nevada. The road travels between the Mojave Desert and the Sierra Nevada's western slope. The seventy-five-mile trip across the mountains gains and loses six thousand feet of elevation. While the drive can be made in a day, hiking and biking trails, campgrounds, and opportunities for fishing offer powerful inducements for a longer visit.

I prefer to begin this trip from the east, on Nine Mile Canyon Road off U.S. Highway 395, about 155 miles north of Los Angeles. I fill my car's tank in the little community of Pearsonville, a few miles south of Nine Mile Canyon Road, because the plateau has no gas stations.

From Pearsonville, there are good views of brown desert peaks, red volcanic cinder cones, and a twenty-thousand-year-old black lava flow to the north. The towns of Ridgecrest and Inyokern lie to the east, in the broad Indian Wells Valley. Settled by pioneers in the nineteenth century, these neighboring high desert towns now serve the nearby China Lake Naval Weapons Center.

Nine Mile Canyon Road heads west toward the rounded, seemingly barren Sierra Nevada foothills, which, on closer inspection, actually reveal a cover of desert grasses and yucca trees, the latter a smaller cousin of the strange Joshua trees. Cottonwoods line the bottom of the canyon where the road crosses a gigantic pipeline, part of the aqueduct that carries water south to Los Angeles. Pull off the road by the pipeline and listen to the resonance of gurgling water as it surges under an air vent.

The road narrows as it climbs. The precipitous drop-offs into Nine Mile Canyon will frighten the faint of heart. A few pullouts offer impressive views east over the receding desert peaks, while the road just climbed can be seen snaking down the canyon. Ahead, higher slopes, topped with jagged peaks, are now dotted with pinyon pines. The road widens, levels out, and changes names, becoming Kennedy Meadows Road. It begins to travel through the mountain meadows and pine forests of Sequoia National Forest.

For the next several miles, the road passes through areas of the seventy-four thousand acres burned in a massive fire in 2000. Where the fire

Start this route 155 miles north of Los Angeles on U.S. Highway 395. A few miles north of Pearsonville, exit west onto Nine Mile Canyon Road (County Road J41). Drive west over the Kern Plateau for seventy-five miles; the road changes names to Kennedy Meadows Road and, farther west, to Sherman Pass Road.

At the junction with the Sierra Highway, turn south to Lake Isabella or north to the San Joaquin Valley.

> *"A high mountain trail through the Sierra had been the unfulfilled dream for decades."*
> —Fredrick Tabor Cooper, *Rider's California, a Guidebook for Travelers, 1925*

A magnificent desert sunrise greets early risers looking east from Nine Mile Canyon toward distant desert peaks.

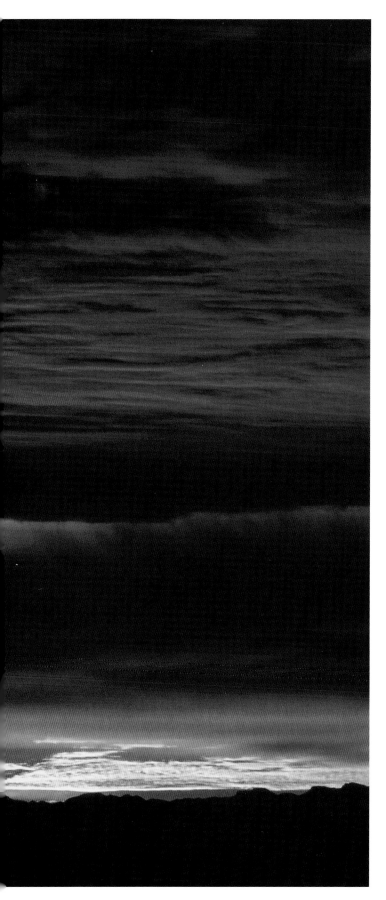

A Collard lizard sits on a rough piece of lava at the base of the Sierra Nevada, not far from the bottom of Nine Mile Canyon.

Wildflowers bloom riotously in the aftermath of a forest fire in Sequoia National Forest.

burned, no trees will grow to substantial size for at least another fifty years, but the scorched earth partially compensates for the loss with showy displays of spring wildflowers.

At Kennedy Meadows, there is a campground, several trails into the wilderness, and the Grumpy Bear Resort, which has a rustic restaurant and rental cabins. The Kennedy Meadows General Store lies a few miles away, near the South Fork of the Kern River. Just to the south, hikers can find a trailhead into Domeland Wilderness, which has thousands of granite domes and spires.

The road changes names again at Kennedy Meadows. Now Sherman Pass Road, it gradually climbs past meadows, campgrounds, trailheads, and views of the High Sierra peaks through breaks in the forest. The road passes Bald Mountain and the Bald Mountain fire lookout. The mountaintop wears the sediments that once overlaid the Sierra Nevada batholith. The sediments, from the floor of an ancient sea, have now almost completely eroded away and are visible in only a few places in the Sierra Nevada.

Sherman Pass is not far from Bald Mountain. The pass, still well below the tree line, is nonetheless ninety-two hundred feet above sea level. (Like the General Sherman Tree in Sequoia National Park, the pass and mountain were named for the Civil War general, William Tecumseh Sherman, who lived in Northern California before the Civil War.) A vista point off the pass offers a good look across the southern Sierra Nevada.

From the pass, the road begins a winding descent through the forest. Some of the terrain that burned during a 2002 fire comes into view. That fire threatened, but ultimately did not burn, several groves of giant sequoias west of the Kern River.

Sherman Pass Road reaches a junction with the Big Meadow Road, which travels south over dirt to the western edge of Domeland Wilderness. Beyond the junction, Sherman Pass Road begins a more earnest descent down the Sierra Nevada's western slopes into the Kern River Canyon. The fire-damaged slopes of oaks and chaparral are left behind by the time the road reaches the Sierra Highway.

From here, the Sierra Highway travels south to popular Lake Isabella in the Kern River Valley. To the north, the highway climbs toward the southernmost groves of giant sequoia trees along the Great Western Divide Highway and a series of backroads that lead into the San Joaquin Valley.

HIGH ADVENTURE
Around Mount Whitney

There is a top-of-world view from the summit of Mount Whitney. But the air at 14,494 feet above sea level is thin, and not everyone can make the 22-mile round-trip hike to the summit. Yet anyone can enjoy splendid views of Mount Whitney, as well as the adjacent High Sierra peaks and

ROUTE 18

Follow Whitney Portal Road west from the town of Lone Pine on U.S. Highway 395. To explore the Alabama Hills, turn left onto Tuttle Creek Road just west of town and drive south. Or turn right onto Movie Ranch Road almost three miles out of town and drive north.

To reach the trailhead to Mount Langley, return to Whitney Portal Road and turn onto Horseshoe Meadow Road, just past the turnoff to Movie Ranch Road. Go twenty miles to the Cottonwood Lakes Trailhead.

To reach the trailhead to Mount Whitney, return to Whitney Portal Road and follow it west to its terminus thirteen miles from Lone Pine.

the impressive Owens Valley, by traveling over a few exciting backroads.

The journey to Mount Whitney begins in Lone Pine. This decidedly unpretentious gateway town, straddling U.S. Highway 395 in the Owens Valley, originally supplied miners and ranchers with provisions. Today, the town serves the tourists who pass through on their way to fish, hunt, ski, climb, and backpack in the Sierra Nevada.

Lone Pine was named for a single tree that stood near the confluence of two creeks. Unlike twenty-seven unlucky inhabitants of the town, the tree managed to survive the great earthquake of 1872. The quake leveled almost every building in town, and the ground shook as far away as San Diego and Sacramento. Just north of Lone Pine, a monument marking the event sits next to a block of earth lifted several feet by the quake. A common grave for sixteen of the victims sits atop the block. While earthquakes occur regularly in California, geologists don't expect a temblor of similar size to recur in Lone Pine for another three thousand years.

"Well seasoned limbs will enjoy the climb of 9000 feet required for this direct route, but soft, succulent people should go the mule way."
—John Muir, *Century Magazine*, 1891

Unlike earthquakes, the Lone Pine Film Festival is an annual event. It attracts thousands of visitors who come to celebrate the hundreds of movies, television shows, and commercials that have been filmed in the area. With Mount Whitney and the High Sierra as an imposing backdrop, the most popular filming locations take place in the nearby Alabama Hills, an enormous area of strangely rounded boulder formations.

The Alabama Hills are the eroded tops of ancient granite bedrock exposed by earthquake faulting. They were named for the Confederate battleship *Alabama* by Southern sympathizers who mined the area in 1863. (When the U.S.S. *Kearsarge* sank the C.S.S. *Alabama,* the nearby town of Independence named a peak, a pass, and a mining camp after the Union ship). Now the federal Bureau of Land Management holds jurisdiction over much of the Alabama Hills.

Western film legends Tom Mix, Roy Rodgers, Gene Autry, Hopalong Cassidy, John Wayne, and Clint Eastwood have all ridden their steeds through the Alabama Hills, and the boulder fields have also appeared in science fiction films and television shows. *The Charge of the Light Brigade* (1936) and *Gunga Din* (1939), two movie classics set in nineteenth-century India, were filmed here. *Gunga Din,* with its spectacular scenery and exciting storyline, served as a major inspiration for the Indiana Jones movies fifty years later.

Several roads travel through the Alabama Hills. Tuttle Creek Road and Movie Ranch Road, both side roads off Whitney Portal Road, are two of the best. Tuttle Creek Road starts just west of Lone Pine and twists and turns its way up, down, and around the hills. Movie Ranch Road, almost three miles west of town, travels past many weathered formations that have served as backdrops for innumerable movies.

Back on Whitney Portal Road, drivers continue toward the flanks of the Sierra Nevada. Mount Whitney was named in 1864 in honor of Josiah Whitney, the leader of the California Geological Survey. In 1873, when

Cowboys still herd cattle along the base of the High Sierra. These cattle will soon cross U.S. Highway 395, south of Lone Pine.

RIGHT:

An old cottonwood tree stands like a sentinel in the Owens Valley.

LEFT:

Minutes after jumping off the edge of a mountain along Horseshoe Meadow Road, a hang glider rises on a warm current of air over the Owens Valley.

BELOW:

Mount Whitney, the highest point in the forty-eight contiguous states and the crest of the High Sierra, is visible through an arch near Movie Flats Road.

Owens Valley fisherman Charley Begole, Johnny Lucas, and Al Johnson became the first men to reach Mount Whitney's summit, local residents vainly attempted to have the mountain officially—and somewhat inelegantly—renamed Fisherman's Peak.

Many others would follow King and the fishermen to climb Mount Whitney, including famed naturalist John Muir, who pioneered the classic "East Face" route enjoyed by generations of mountaineers, including myself.

Continuing up Whitney Portal Road, the desert is soon left behind as pinyon pines take the place of sagebrush. At the first switchback, stop for a pullout with a terrific view looking east across the Owens Valley; the Alabama Hills lie far below and the Argus Mountains make up the horizon. Drivers will see some grand views of the summit of Mount Whitney itself as the road turns a corner farther up. Whitney Portal Road ends eighty-three hundred feet above sea level and thirteen miles west of Lone Pine. The trail to the summit of Mount Whitney's begins here, beckoning climbers and backpackers. But the trailhead itself, in a pine forest surrounded by granite cliffs, is a fitting destination for a backroad explorer.

Horseshoe Meadow Road, an alternative route into the High Sierra, also takes off from Whitney Portal Road, just past Movie Ranch Road. It has some precipitous drop-offs and glorious views of the Owens Valley over the course of twenty miles, until the road ends at the Cottonwood Lakes trailhead and a pack station. The altitude at the end of the road is a literally breathtaking 10,090 feet above sea level. The trail leads into the Sierra Nevada backcountry below the summit of 14,049-foot Mount Langley, the peak Clarence King accidentally climbed back in 1871. The peak was named for Samuel Pierpont Langley, an astronomer and physicist who conducted research on solar heat from the top of Mount Whitney. In 1896, Langley also built an airplane powered by a steam engine that flew for ninety seconds over the Potomac River, in Virginia. Although it flew without a human at the controls, it was the first flight of an engine-powered aircraft. Unlike the Wright brothers, Langley was never able to master the principals of flight control.

It is ironic, then, that the road up to Horseshoe Meadow includes a view of one of the world's premier hang-gliding launch spots. Intrepid pilots take off next to the road from a place called Walt's Point, nine thousand feet in elevation. Tethered beneath a rigid wing covered with colorful nylon or Mylar, the glider pilots launch in the morning, as the sun begins to create rising currents of warming air. Imagine if professor Langley could visit the launch point today on the flanks of the mountain named in his honor. He would watch the daring pilots in their engineless crafts, easily controling their gliders as they climb into the thin air high above Mount Whitney to enjoy the splendid, top-of-the-world view.

Errol Flynn leads the troops in the 1936 film epic Charge of the Light Brigade. *This movie, like countless others, was shot in the scenic Alabama Hills, not far from the little town of Lone Pine. (Courtesy of the Lone Pine Chamber of Commerce)*

PART V

THE MOJAVE DESERT

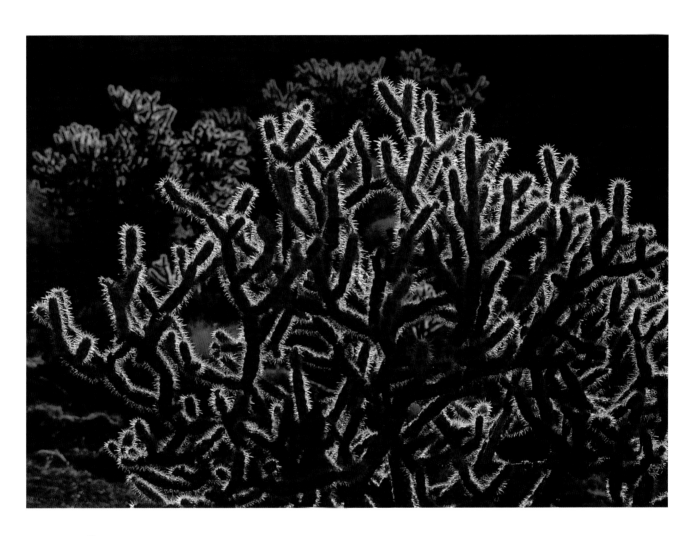

FACING PAGE:

The Salt Creek oasis sits at the base of the rugged Tucki Mountains. An impermeable layer of rocks here blocks the normal underground flow of water through this portion of Death Valley, meager though it may be, forcing the water to the surface.

ABOVE:

The rising sun illuminates cactus needles in the Mojave National Preserve.

Aridity defines the Mojave Desert, but there are few other unifying characteristics in this diverse landscape.

The Mojave Desert includes the lowest point of elevation in the United States, at Badwater in Death Valley National Park. Death Valley is also home to over a thousand species of plants, some found only within the park confines.

The creosote bush is common to all the deserts of North America, including the Mojave. But the creosote is unique, too, because it is the longest-lived thing in the world. The seeds of one specimen in the Mojave Desert apparently germinated at the close of the last ice age, almost twelve thousand years ago. The Mojave Desert is home to another, less common plant, the strangely shaped Joshua tree. While these trees—actually a giant form of the yucca plant—grow in Nevada and Arizona, they are most numerous in California's Joshua Tree National Park. The park also contains thousands of acres of fantastic boulder fields.

The Mojave National Preserve lies between Death Valley and Joshua Tree National Parks. Here, the backroads travel to cinder cones, limestone caverns, some of North America's highest sand dunes, and a historic railroad depot.

There are mountains in the desert that rise high enough to receive significant rainfall and snowfall. And while summer temperatures at low elevations can reach over 120 degrees, winter temperatures at high elevations can drop below the freezing point.

The word "Mojave" means "beside the water" in the language of the Mojave people, who lived along the Colorado River. The Mojave Desert is mostly dry, but it is also home to numerous hot springs, underground rivers, and the occasional oasis.

Here, coyotes sometimes boldly step into the middle of a road, stopping traffic and hoping for handouts from sympathetic tourists. Sidewinders slither over sand dunes and bighorn sheep clamber over rocky peaks. Desert tortoises slowly make their way past cactus groves. Canyon walls echo with the braying of burros, descendants of pack animals turned loose more than a century ago by miners who gave up the search for gold.

Most American Indians were forced from their desert lands by the miners and pioneers who arrived in the nineteenth century. But the newcomers sometimes proved less hardy than their predecessors. The landscape offers ample evidence of more recent human incursions that failed to take root in the Mojave Desert, especially along the old highways that used to serve as major routes west. These highways are littered with the ruins of roadhouses, motor courts, and gas stations that once served as cultural icons for social and technological progress.

Multilane interstates carry most of the traffic through the Mojave Desert these days. But the most interesting and diverse places can only be reached along the backroads.

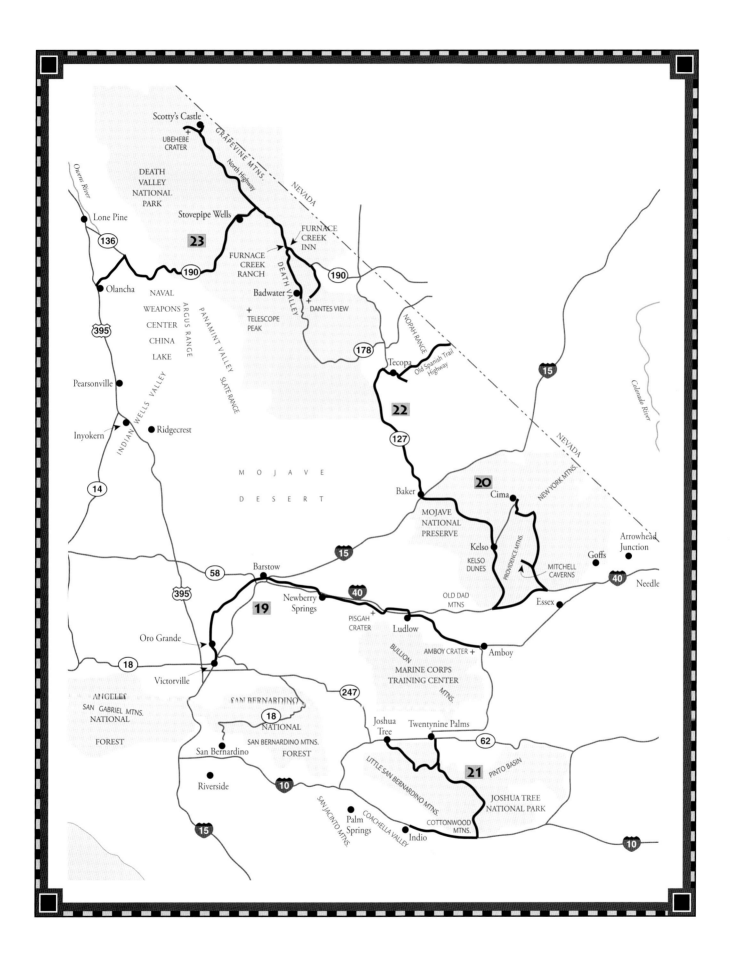

Bottle art decorates the front yard of a home along Route 66, between the cities of Victorville and Barstow.

A customized license plate adorns the front of a 1960 Nash Rambler permanently parked at the classic Route 66 Motel. The motel was reputedly built in 1929, making it the oldest motor court in the town of Barstow.

Morning sun shines on Roy's Motel and Café after a brief winter rainstorm.

Tom's Welding, in Barstow, boasts a collection of gas station and Route 66 signs.

An old service station in Newberry Springs no longer has any gas to sell. Judging from the price on the pump, the station has been closed for a long time.

HISTORIC ROUTE 66
From Victorville to Amboy

ROUTE 19

From Interstate 15 at Victorville, take the Palmdale Road exit and follow the Route 66 signs along Seventh Street to D Street. Turn left and follow signs onto the National Trails Highway, which is also signed as Route 66. This highway runs north through Oro Grande and then turns east toward Barstow.

From Barstow, follow Interstate 40 east, then regain Route 66 a few miles later as a frontage road. Go twenty miles to Newberry Springs. To reach the Pisgah Crater, follow the frontage road another ten miles east, then turn right onto Hector Road. Back on the frontage road, drive ten miles east to Ludlow. From here, leave Interstate 40 and follow Route 66 signs southeast to Amboy.

To return to Interstate 40, follow Route 66 another thirty-two miles east. Or, to reach the town of Twentynine Palms and Joshua Tree National Park, follow Amboy Road fifty miles south.

Some of the Mojave Desert landscape along famed Route 66 is spectacular, but scenery is not the primary reason for exploring the old highway. The road itself and the colorful cultural debris along it are the real draws.

Long ago, Route 66 was not a backroad. It was "The Mother Road" and "America's Main Street." Created by an act of Congress in 1926, Route 66 connected a series of roads that led for 2,448 miles from Chicago to Los Angeles. The new route led successive waves of travelers west. Among them were Dust Bowl refugees of the Great Depression. Next came World War II veterans and their families. In 1946, songwriter Bobby Troup wrote "Route 66," which became the highway's theme song after Nat King Cole recorded it that same year. That song came out precisely when tourists, who formed the last great wave of travelers, began to get their kicks on Route 66.

The highway ended its unbroken run in 1985, when workers completed Interstate 40 and decommissioned the last stretch of the old highway. Now Route 66 exists as a series of segmented backroads. Even so, interest in the famous roadway has never faded. Evoking a powerful sense of nostalgia, new "Historic Route 66" highway signs have sprouted along much of the old road and colorful neon still lights the way to old motor courts and diners.

In California, Route 66 cruises for 320 miles between the Colorado River, near the town of Needles, and the Santa Monica Pier, at the Pacific Ocean. During the heyday of Route 66, most travelers drove from east to west. But our tour reverses the direction, traveling from the city of Victorville to the community at Amboy.

The starting point is the Palmdale Road exit off Interstate 15, in Victorville. Named for a Santa Fe Railroad superintendent in 1885, Victorville is a medium-sized but fast-growing town eighty-five miles east of Los Angeles. The highway follows its original path along Seventh Street in Old Town Victorville to D Street, where the California Route 66 Museum celebrates the highway's heritage.

Crossing under Interstate 15, D Street continues both as Route 66 and as the National Trails Highway. Beyond Victorville, the highway runs north along the usually dry Mojave River, where massive cement factories have replaced the failed dreams of nineteenth-century gold miners. The San Gabriel Mountains, snowcapped in winter, serve as a backdrop to the west.

Route 66 turns east and passes by the ruins of old stores, a post office, service stations, and auto courts. Watch for the "Bottle House" on the west side of the highway, where hundreds of colorful old bottles hang on scores of poles that look like tall hat racks.

The drive offers expansive views across the desert as Route 66 reaches Main Street in the city of Barstow. An important junction for centuries— first for American Indians, then Spanish explorers and American pioneers—Barstow today is the western terminus of Interstate 40. It also serves as the eastern end of California Highway 58, which links the desert with the San Joaquin Valley to the west. Interstate 15 continues east into Nevada and serves as the major weekend route for Californians headed to Las Vegas.

Like Victorville, Barstow was named for a railroad superintendent; it is home to the enormous Burlington Vermont–Santa Fe rail yard. Casa Desierto, a "Harvey House" established by entrepreneur Fred Harvey, was built in 1911; it sits a couple blocks off Main Street. It was one of the many Harvey Houses that served as dining rooms and boardinghouses along the Santa Fe Railroad line. Long abandoned, Casa Desierto was renovated in the 1990s, and now houses the Amtrak station, the Mother Road Route 66 Museum, and the Western America Railroad Museum.

Main Street leads past a cornucopia of fast food restaurants, gas stations, and motels. The Route 66 Motel, one of the town's original motor courts, boasts a spectacular neon sign and a collection of old cars and other Route 66 artifacts. Beyond the town, Route 66 is temporarily submerged by Interstate 40 and resurfaces a few miles later as a rough frontage road. Desert mountains now closely flank the south side of the road. About twenty miles past Barstow, the frontage road veers north into the little community of Newberry Springs. The Bagdad Cafe, where the 1987 cult movie of the same name was filmed, draws visitors from around the world. The food is delicious and some of the locals, who enjoyed playing bit parts in the film, frequent the café.

The Pisgah Crater, a cinder cone estimated to have erupted less than one hundred thousand years ago, lies about ten miles east of Newberry Springs. It can be reached by taking the exit for Hector Road off either Interstate 40 or the Route 66 frontage road. Some of the cone has been removed to make roadbeds for train tracks, but active mining seems to have stopped. Travelers can drive a passenger car almost to the top of the cone, and the short walk to the summit offers a spectacular 360-degree view of the surrounding desert. Explore the east side of the crater to find numerous lava tubes, some of which extend several yards in length and are large enough to stand up in. Other tubes are just large enough to wriggle through.

About ten miles past Pisgah, Route 66 takes leave of Interstate 40 at Ludlow. This little community features a couple gas stations, a café, a pleasant motel, and some deserted buildings. The next reliable services are about eighty miles east; top off the gas tank here.

A vast open desert valley runs between the Bullion Mountains to the south and the Old Dad Mountains to the north. After thirty miles, the Amboy Crater, another cinder cone, comes into view. A rough road leads to the base of cone, and a short but steep trail leads to the summit.

The tiny community of Amboy lies about ten miles beyond the cinder cone. At one time, Amboy functioned as a major rest stop along Route

The Spanish mission–style Kelso train depot, restored to its 1924 glory, serves as the visitor center for the Mojave National Preserve.

Cacti bloom during the spring in the Mojave National Preserve.

When it rains, the barrel cactus can expand its sponge-like tissue to soak up and store water. While Native Americans ate the fruit and seeds of the barrel cactus, the belief that it can be broken open to obtain drinking water is a myth.

An abandoned homestead slowly disintegrates in the desert sun at the community of Cima.

66. Today only Roy's Motel and Café, opened in 1937, and its gas station, a few motel units, and a '50s-style diner remain to provide sporadic services to visitors. In the late 1950s, Roy's received a towering new sign and a new building to house the motel lobby. These modern-looking structures are examples of Southern California's classic Astro—or Googie—architecture, which attempted to mimic the technological designs of the then-new space age.

A few miles south of town, on Amboy Road, the National Chloride Company mines salt for industrial uses. Watch for piles of dirt the size of apartment buildings and for huge trenches gouged into salt flats on the west side of the road.

Amboy is a fitting place to end our Route 66 tour, because it is easy enough to return within a few hours to Barstow, Victorville, or even Los Angeles. But Amboy can also serve as a crossroads, offering drivers several options for further exploration. For example, continuing along Route 66 another thirty-two miles east leads past more ruined outposts of civilization, as well as through the minuscule communities of Essex, Goffs, and Searchlight Junction, before rejoining Interstate 40 near the California-Arizona border.

Amboy Road heads south for fifty miles through the sparsely populated Wonder Valley until it reaches the town of Twentynine Palms, next to Joshua Tree National Park. Kelbaker Road, a few miles east of Amboy, leads straight back to Interstate 40.

WHERE THE BANSHEE DWELLS
The Mojave National Preserve

ROUTE 20

At Baker on Interstate 15, enter the Mojave National Preserve via Kelbaker Road. Go south through Kelso to Interstate 40 on the southern boundary of the preserve. Head east on Interstate 40 and turn north onto either Essex Road to reach the Mitchell Caverns National Preserve or Black Canyon Road to reach the Hole-in-the-Wall Campground. From the campground, explore the preserve on Wildhorse Canyon Road or follow Black Canyon Road north to Cima.

The eastern Mojave Desert, along California's border with Nevada, presents a diverse and remote landscape. The state and federal governments have set aside large areas to preserve vast tracts of wild land and the artifacts of human history. They cobbled together the Mojave National Preserve in 1994 from a number of protected state and federal lands. Interstate 10 bounds the northern side of the preserve, and Interstate 40, the southern side. A vast, open terrain buffers the preserve to the east and west.

This arid preserve contains 1.6 million acres of desert, where travelers can explore giant sand dunes, Joshua trees, cacti, cinder cones, caverns, historic buildings, and barren mountain ranges. Relatively few permanent residents live here, and the preserve offers almost no services, except for the post office and the intermittently open general store in the community of Cima.

The main paved routes, each departing from Interstate 15, include Cima, Kelbaker, and Morning Star Roads. But most roads in the preserve are dirt and often impassible during and after rainstorms or, at higher elevations, snowfall. And while some of the most interesting places to visit in the preserve are reasonably close together, they are not necessarily on or even connected by paved roads.

Kelbaker Road runs through the western portion of the preserve through the community of Kelso. Named for a railroad employee, Kelso was founded in 1906 as a railway stop for trains running between Los Angeles and Salt Lake City. The old steam engines needed a full tank of water and extra locomotives to help make the steep climb up the nearby Cima Grade.

The beautiful, Spanish mission–style Kelso Depot, was built in 1924. By the 1940s, it served a community of almost two thousand people, including railroad employees and miners. More than twenty-five hundred tons of iron ore were shipped each day to the Kaiser Steel Mill in the city of Fontana, east of Los Angeles. When mining operations ceased and diesel engines replaced steam locomotives, the town withered. The depot closed and faced demolition. Fortunately, determined opposition saved the old building, which now serves as the preserve's information center.

The Kelso Dunes are not far from the depot. These dunes are among the largest in Southern California; in places, wind has blown the sand into ridges six hundred feet high. A rough dirt road a few miles south of the depot leads to an information kiosk and a trail into the dunes.

The Mitchell Caverns Natural Preserve is located at forty-three hundred feet above sea level, in the Providence Mountains. It's on Essex Road, fifteen miles north of Interstate 40. The caverns, which contain an unusual array of rare formations, as well as stalactites and stalagmites, formed between 12 and 15 million years ago.

The caverns were named for Jack and Ida Mitchell. The couple came to the Providence Mountains in 1932 to look for silver but discovered more profit was to be made showing off the caverns. They opened a small resort that operated for more than twenty years. California purchased the caverns for the park system in 1954. The park offers tours daily except in the summer months, when the caverns are open only on the weekends. Six campsites, available near the entrance to the caverns, offer a wonderful view of the desert far below.

Travelers can set up camp in one of thirty-five primitive sites at Hole-in-the-Wall Campground, accessible on unpaved Black Canyon Road ten miles past Essex Road and the turnoff to Mitchell Caverns. The campground sits at the base of a wall of rock, lava, and ash deposited after a volcanic eruption ten million years ago. Wind, water, and frost have worked on the iron compounds in the volcanic sediments to create innumerable holes as well as a palette of warm hues. The landscape here is treeless but filled with many species of cacti.

A nearby trail leads into Banshee Canyon, supposedly named for the weird sounds that issue from it when the wind blows through. The trail itself is only a few hundred yards in length, and the way through it is

"The Mojave Desert has an evil reputation. All over the West, its name conjures up a picture of scorched and empty wilderness, implacably hostile to man."
—Colin Fletcher,
The Thousand Mile Summer

Palms and cottonwoods decorate the low-desert landscape at Cottonwood Spring, near the south boundary of Joshua Tree National Park. Native Americans and miners historically used the spring.

Mormon pioneers thought the Joshua tree looked like the biblical figure Joshua, pointing the way to the Promised Land with his outstretched arms.

A climber rappels down a rope after successfully ascending a cliff near the campground at Hidden Valley.

A yucca, similar to the Joshua tree but consisting of a single branch, is in full bloom at the White Tank campground, in the upper reaches of Joshua Tree National Park.

quite steep near its eastern entrance. Large metal rings secured to the rock aid passage down the narrow chute.

From the campground, Black Canyon Road leads to higher elevations towards a forest of Joshua trees and the paved road at Cima.

STRANGE GARDENS
Joshua Tree National Park

ROUTE 21

To enter Joshua Tree National Park from the north, take California Highway 62 to the village of Joshua Tree or the town of Twentynine Palms. Drive south from either town on Park Boulevard.

About a mile a half west of Jumbo Rocks Campground, Geology Tour Road travels south off Park Boulevard. Keys View Road is about two miles west of the turnoff to the Ryan campground and Ryan Mountain trailhead.

To enter the park from the south, take Interstate 10 twenty-five miles east from the city of Indio. Turn left onto Pinto Basin Road, not far from Cottonwood Spring.

Park Boulevard is an odd name for the road that traverses much of Joshua Tree National Park. The word "boulevard" ordinarily conjures a broad thoroughfare and an artificially decorated landscape. But the road that runs through the park from the town of Joshua Tree to the town of Twentynine Palms is narrow, and the landscape on either side is completely and stunningly natural.

Located a few hours east of the city of Los Angeles, Joshua Tree National Park straddles portions of the Mojave and Colorado Desert environments. The park is home to the Joshua tree itself, a tree-like member of the lily family of plants. It grows only in the Mojave Desert. Its trunk, which stands between fifteen and forty feet tall, is crowned with a multitude of crooked branches, which are in turn covered with leaves that have been likened to long daggers. In the spring, the plants sport large, greenish-white, bell-shaped flowers.

In order for this giant plant to reproduce, it needs to be pollinated. That only happens when a species of the night-flying female Pronuba moth deposits a load of pollen on the Joshua tree's flowers. Without that moth, the plant would be doomed. By the same token, the moth depends on the Joshua tree for its own survival, for that is the only plant on which it will lay its eggs.

According to legend, Mormon pioneers traveling from Salt Lake City to the town of San Bernardino gave the Joshua tree its name. Its branches, like the outstretched arms of the Old Testament prophet, Joshua, seemed to beckon the Mormons toward the Promised Land.

Joshua Tree National Park is also home to spectacular desert geology. The landscape along Park Boulevard abounds with dramatic cliffs and giant boulders, often piled atop one another. The rough granite rocks are laced with vertical cracks, or slots, that makes this land a favorite haunt of rock climbers. The cliffs and boulders formed millions of years ago, after molten rock pushed up from beneath the earth's surface.

The park offers more than just scenery. It also offers some 500 archeological sites, 88 historic structures, and a park museum with a collection of 123,253 items. Many of these items, including clothing, baskets and pots, and hunting implements, are associated with American Indians, who for thousands of years moved freely within the area that now makes up the park's nearly eight hundred thousand acres.

Some American Indians lived at a place they called "Mar-rah," or "the place of little springs and much grass," on what today is the north-eastern edge of the park. This oasis was renamed Twentynine Palms in 1855 by the first whites to survey and write about the area, its native people, and the surrounding desert lands. The Oasis of Mara, as it is called today, exists because an earthquake fault has allowed subterranean waters to rise to the surface of the desert. Today, the Oasis of Mara still supports a grove of palms and is on the grounds of the park's visitor center. Five other palm oases are located in the park.

By 1913, the tribes were gone from their oasis, their place taken by cattle ranchers. Later, veterans of World War I who had been gassed came to Twentynine Palms, believing the warm climate would aid in their recovery.

Joshua Tree became a national monument in 1936; in turn, the monument became a national park in 1994. With the park headquarters and visitor center built on the site of the oasis, the town of Twentynine Palms grew to serve the needs of the park's visitors. It also serves the U.S. Marine Corps Air Ground Combat Center just north of the town. The city calls itself the Oasis of Murals because outdoor murals decorate entire walls on many commercial buildings. The colorful murals celebrate the town's cultural and natural history.

Beyond the visitor center, Park Boulevard climbs quickly into the higher reaches of the park and the Mojave Desert, then turns abruptly right, running across the rocky spine of Joshua Tree National Park all the way into the town of Joshua Tree, to the northwest. Along the way, it passes cliffs and boulders at Jumbo Rocks, Wonderland of Rocks, and Hidden Valley. Hiking trails lead to places like the Desert Queen and Lost Horse mines, and to Barker Dam, built by cowboys in the nineteenth century. Visitors sometimes see bighorn sheep gathering early in the morning to drink from the reservoir. Coyotes, black-tailed jackrabbits, birds, lizards, kangaroo rats, and caterpillars also inhabit the park.

While Park Boulevard is the main route through Joshua Tree, other roads run through the park. Keys View Road leads to the Keys View. Massive Mount San Jacinto looms in the south. Geology Tour Road offers a self-guided tour of Pleasant Valley.

Pinto Basin Road leaves the Mojave Desert to descend into the Colorado Desert. Here, the Joshua trees disappear, their place taken by the creosote bush, the ocotillo, and various species of cactus. The Cholla Cactus Garden, right off Pinto Basin Road, contains a stand of cacti more than five feet tall.

Not far from the park's southern boundary, the road passes by Cottonwood Spring. Historically, the Cahuilla collected fresh water from this pristine spring, which lies near the ruins of three gold mines. Visitors can spot birds and bighorn sheep at the area's cottonwoods and palms, planted at the spring in the 1920s.

Beyond Cottonwood Spring, Pinto Basin Road leads to Interstate 10. The cities of Indio and Palm Springs, in the Coachella Valley, lie to the west. The interstate promises a quick return to civilization. But because

> *"The most repulsive tree in the vegetable kingdom."*
> —John C. Frémont, *The Exploring Expedition to the Rocky Mountains, Oregon and California*, 1852

Amargosa Canyon was created at least five hundred thousand years ago, when the ancestral Lake Tecopa overflowed its banks and carved out the dramatic landscape we see today.

of its long history and pre-history, its strange rock formations, wildflowers, oases, and its "repulsive" Joshua trees, the desert world will not soon fade from memory.

PUPFISH AND DATE SHAKES
Tecopa Hot Springs and the Old Spanish Trail

ROUTE 22

From the town of Baker on Interstate 15, take California Highway 127 north fifty miles to the community of Tecopa. Turn right onto Old Spanish Trail Highway and then left onto Hot Springs Road to explore Tecopa. Or stay on Old Spanish Trail to Furnace Creek Road, then turn right and head south to China Ranch and the California–Nevada border.

John C. Frémont, "the Pathfinder," made five expeditions to the American West. His published reports made for popular reading across the United Sates. Among his many notable achievements and failures, Frémont became the first Republican candidate to run for the presidency; he lost to the Democrat, Millard Fillmore. (Courtesy of the Library of Congress.)

Long before interstate highways, before Route 66, before automobiles, and while California was still part of Mexico, the American continent was linked from east to west by the Old Spanish Trail. The trail began as a trade route, and it became a place where the cultures of native peoples and newcomers, both Spanish and American, merged.

First scouted by Spanish explorers, the trail gained notoriety between 1829 and 1848, when Mexican and American traders brought woolen blankets and clothing west by mule train from New Mexico to Los Angeles. Then they retraced their way, bringing back horses and mules to sell in New Mexico and Missouri.

One historian deemed the original trail "the longest, crookedest, most arduous pack mule route in the history of America." Today, it's easy to explore portions of the Old Spanish Trail near the California and Nevada border. The place to start is the low-desert community of Tecopa, just off of California Highway 127, north of the town of Baker and Interstate 15.

The Amargosa River, which normally runs beneath the desert, sometimes surfaces near Tecopa. Little Grimshaw Lake—really a marsh—is just north of town. There are several marshes in the area, as well as hot springs. The county-run Tecopa Hot Springs serves as the focal point for an adjacent seasonal community of mobile home residents. The county hot springs have "his" and "her" bathhouses that are anything but fancy, but that's part of their charm. A few commercial resorts cater to visitors, too.

Tecopa is home to an endangered species of desert pupfish. During the last ice age, perhaps thirty to sixty thousand years ago, ancestors of the pupfish lived in lakes and rivers in the southwest. As the glaciers retreated and the land became arid, these silver-colored fish, which grow to about 2.5 inches, were able to adapt and survive in the isolated hot springs, marshes, and intermittent creeks of the Mojave Desert. The pupfish at Tecopa can be found in the marshes and hot pools on Furnace Creek Road, just north of town, and at the Delight's Hot Springs Resort.

The human history of Tecopa is of more recent vintage. The Mexican horse trader Antonio Armijo passed through the area in the spring of 1830, looking for the easiest route to Los Angeles. He found about seventy Piute people living at the hot springs; they called their winter village Yaga. The Piutes were eventually displaced from their lands. But the village of Yaga would be renamed Tecopa, in honor of the Piute leader who first fought against and then sought mutual accommodation among his people, the miners, and the ranchers who laid claim to the land.

Explorer John C. Frémont led five expeditions into the western portion of North America. On his second expedition, in 1844, Frémont traveled over a portion of the Old Spanish Trail. He wrote about coming upon the scene of an ambush of horse traders by American Indians just east of Tecopa. He also wrote about two survivors, including an eleven-year-old boy, Pablo Hernandez.

Frémont's scout, Kit Carson, was already famous in his own right; he and another scout, Alexander Godey, left the expedition to recover the horses. According to Frémont, the scouts returned with the horses and two scalps. Frémont brought Pablo, whose parents died in the massacre, back to Washington, where the boy was raised by the family of Frémont's wife, Jessie. According to Frémont, Pablo returned to California as an adult and became an outlaw.

The delightful China Ranch, just south of Tecopa, is a date ranch and an oasis. The road to the oasis drops without warning into a deeply eroded wash to end in a valley filled with date palms and hemmed in by chalky badlands. Over the years, the valley has served variously as a cattle ranch and as a hog, alfalfa, and fig farm. The date trees were planted from seeds in the 1920s. The ranch today includes a store with dates, muffins, cookies, and nut breads, and the owners encourage visitors to explore the oasis on foot or by car.

Sometime before the turn of the twentieth century, a Chinese man took up residence in the oasis. He supplied mining camps with fresh vegetables, fruits, and meat. The man's name is not known for sure, but his land would become known as China Ranch. Today, the land belongs to the Brown family, descendants of Charles Brown, a Mojave Desert pioneer and longtime state senator.

Tecopa and China Ranch demonstrate how people have changed the landscape. East of Tecopa, on the Old Spanish Trail Highway, the road runs through the Nopah Mountains Wilderness. Beyond the Nopahs, the road crosses the border into Nevada. The land on both sides of the mountains looks the same as it did before the arrival of American Indians. There are no resorts, homes, ranches, or fences. There is only the narrow ribbon of asphalt road to prove the existence of the modern world.

It's No Mirage
Death Valley National Park

The nineteenth-century guidebook author J. W. Buel may have never visited Death Valley. His descriptions of Death Valley mirages are pure inventions. We do know the first visitors to explore that immense and unearthly basin viewed no mirages. These visitors—American Indians—discovered real lakes, a pleasant climate, and plentiful game. But over the past four thousand years, Death Valley began to slowly dry out, until it became a seemingly desolate wasteland.

> *"The dead silence of the place was ominous and galloping rapidly up, we found only the corpses of the two men; everything else was gone."*
> —John C. Frémont, *The Exploring Expedition to the Rocky Mountains, Oregon and California*, 1852

ROUTE 23

From U.S. Highway 395 at Olancha, drive east on California Highway 190. Follow it into Death Valley National Park and northeast through the community of Stovepipe Wells.

Five miles beyond Stovepipe Wells, Highway 190 reaches a junction with North Highway. Turn left to follow North Highway northwest to Ubehebe Crater and Scotty's Castle. Or turn right to follow Highway 190 southeast to the park visitor center in the community of Furnace Creek. Salt Creek is off Highway 190, between Stovepipe Wells and Furnace Creek.

From Furnace Creek, follow California Highway 178 south to Badwater. Or travel east on Highway 190 to Dante's View Road; Highway 190 continues east to California Highway 127. Interstate 15 is to the south.

During the winter and spring, a surprising amount of rainwater and snowmelt percolates through the mountains to reach the floor of Death Valley, much of which lies below sea level.

There is a separate, usually invisible world in Death Valley: the one at our feet. This tiny, yellow spider, its body less than a quarter-inch across, lives beneath the petals of a flower that may not bloom for years. Where the spider lives or what color it may be when the flower is not in bloom is a mystery.

A sidewinder slithers across footprints in the sand near Stovepipe Wells.

The towers and tile roofs in Death Valley can only belong to the fantastic and legendary Scotty's Castle, which sits high in Grapevine Canyon.

The wind has blown the previous day's footprints off the sand dunes on the west side of Death Valley.

The first white people who found their way into Death Valley certainly described it as a desert. They arrived in 1849 by accident, looking for a shortcut to the California gold fields. Lost and out of food, the forty-niners barely managed to escape the arid basin. Topping a ridge in the Panamint Mountains, William Lewis Manley, who served as a scout and hunter for the group, wrote, "We took off our hats, and then overlooking the scene of so much travail, suffering and death, spoke the thought uppermost, saying Goodbye, Death Valley."

Much of Death Valley is devoid of vegetation, making its colorful geology easily and spectacularly visible. Mustard and Golden Canyons are self-descriptive. Zabriskie Point overlooks deeply eroded mud hills. The Devil's Golf Course contains tiny pinnacles of salt that rise through capillary action from mud just below the surface of Death Valley. As they expand and contract in the desert sun, the tiny salt crystals break apart with a barely audible "plinking" sound.

In some years, rain does not fall on the valley floor. But rainfall and snowfall in the surrounding mountains can be abundant. In rare years, runoff from these mountains can even create an enormous lake in the center of the valley. The lake, only a few inches deep, spreads out for hundreds of acres over the salt flats.

Death Valley is not as lifeless as its name would suggest. True, the thousands of acres of salt flats, where insects are sometimes preserved as tiny mummies, are sterile. Summer temperatures can approach 130 degrees. But the valley is home to a variety of bird life, from ravens that soar over the valley to roadrunners that occasionally dash across the highway. Wildflowers can adorn the valley floor and side canyons; tiny spiders live beneath the flowers. Coyotes and bobcats stalk several species of rodents. Pupfish live in the Salt Creek oasis, and sidewinders slither over the gigantic sand dunes. Death Valley has a human population, too, living in small communities such as Stovepipe Wells. The town has motel, campground, gas station, and small market.

The park's boundaries encompass almost 3.3 million acres in both the basin and the surrounding mountains. In the basin, 550 square miles are below sea level, including the famous little pool at Badwater; at minus 289 feet, it is the lowest place a car can be driven in the Western Hemisphere. Telescope Peak, on the west side of the valley, stands at 11,049 feet above sea level, its summit often mantled with snow.

Given the park's size, it has relatively few roads. California Highway 190 enters from the west and travels south through the heart of the valley before turning east just past the Furnace Creek area. The visitor center, campgrounds, and a motel are located here. The Timbisha Shoshone people, descendants of American Indians who moved into Death Valley more than a thousand years ago, live in a small community just south of the motel.

The West Side Road, which begins south of Furnace Creek, off paved California Highway 178 (also called the Badwater Road), travels over

sometimes-rough dirt and sees little traffic. The junction with North Highway is about seven miles east of Stovepipe Wells. The highway heads towards massive Ubehebe Crater and Scotty's Castle.

Scotty's Castle is a fantastically ornate Spanish-
Moorish style villa in the high desert, tucked into
Grapevine Canyon near the park's northern border.
There are scores of rooms, a series of turrets, and intri-
cate tile designs. According to legend, it was built in
the late 1920s by Walter Scott with funds from a se-
cret gold mine. Better known as Death Valley Scotty,
he was without question the park's most famous deni-
zen. Scotty was also a self-confessed con man with a
national reputation for self-promotion.

In truth, Scotty had charmed the castle's true
owner, Walter Johnson, into playing along with the
charade about the profitable gold mine. Johnson, a
wealthy insurance executive from Chicago, was building the mansion as a vacation home for himself and his

*Death Valley Scotty, loveable con
man and raconteur, poses on his
mule. (Courtesy of the National
Park Service)*

wife. Johnson allowed Scotty to live there but funded the villa's construction, at least until the stock market crash of 1929. Scotty's Castle was never
completed, although this is not apparent to the casual eye. After Johnson
and his wife moved into the castle, Scotty moved nearby into a rustic
cabin. Only after the death of the Johnsons did Scotty return to live in the
castle, in 1951; he died a few years later and was buried on a hill above the
castle. Always a popular attraction, Scotty's Castle was purchased by the
park service in 1970.

The community of Furnace Creek, at the junction of California Highways 178 and 190, is the nerve center of the park; it has the park's headquarters and visitor center, accommodations, and campgrounds. Furnace
Creek can be crowded and its commercial venues might seem spread over
half of Death Valley. For a humbling sense of scale, drive up Dante's View
Road, off Highway 190. Evidence of human presence in the valley is almost invisible from this viewpoint, nearly a mile above sea level.

Most visitors don't bother with the oasis at Salt Creek. Perhaps the
dirt road leading to the oasis keeps them away. The road is reached from
Highway 190, between Stovepipe Wells and Furnace Creek. A short walk
along the boardwalk keeps visitors off the fragile edge of the creek, lined
with salt grass and pickle weed. Beyond the boardwalk, a faint trail follows along Salt Creek as it runs between two lines of mud hills, below the
deeply eroded Tucki Mountains. There are small, dark pools of water here
with darting pupfish. Sometimes, particularly in the morning, great blue
herons and egrets visit the pools. Rarely are there people. Those who have
been there know that Salt Creek and Death Valley are far more wonderful
than any invented description.

PART VI

THE SOUTHERN MOUNTAINS AND DESERTS

FACING PAGE:

Mesa Grande Road, just off California Highway 79 and close to the Santa Isabel Mission, offers a scenic route into the backcountry of San Diego County.

ABOVE:

The yellow-leafed brittlebush and glowing teddy-bear cholla grow in profusion along County Road S3 in Anza-Borrego National Park, near the campground at Tamarisk Grove. The cholla looks soft enough to pet, but this cactus actually sports a dense mass of sharp spines.

The southernmost realm of California is both scenic and sparsely populated. Here are the San Jacinto, Santa Rosa, and Laguna Mountains, all part of the Peninsular Ranges. These mountains lie at the northern end of the Baja California peninsula and have been uplifted along a series of earthquake faults, many of which still generate activity. While the Peninsular Ranges cover an enormous area, individual mountain ranges are fairly small and can be explored in as little as a day over their respective backroads.

Generations of humans—including American Indians, Spanish explorers, and American pioneers—have all explored and settled in these mountains. Many foothills of the Peninsular Ranges have been commercially developed, and housing tracts march up the flanks of some of the mountains. The popular Palm Springs Aerial Tramway was opened in 1963; its intrusion into the wilderness generated some controversy. The tram travels from the desert floor to the higher reaches of Mount San Jacinto, the second highest peak south of the Sierra Nevada Range. The Palomar Observatory, atop Palomar Mountain, houses its famous two-hundred-inch telescope. Little resort communities like Idyllwild and Julian have attracted visitors for well more than a century.

But despite the development, significant portions of the Peninsular Ranges—from the grasslands and oak groves at the base of the mountains to the forested high country—have been protected in state and federal parklands.

To the east, the same forces that lifted the mountains helped create the Colorado Desert, which lies in the "rain shadow" of the Peninsular Ranges. The Colorado Desert, part of the larger Sonora Desert, is named for the Colorado River Delta. This basin is low desert and lies at the southern end of the Salton Trough, a long valley that sinks as much as 180 feet below sea level. The lowest point of the valley is covered by the Salton Sea, created in 1905 when an irrigation canal ruptured along the Mexican border. One of the best places to explore the Colorado Desert is in Anza-Borrego Desert State Park, at the eastern base of the Peninsular Ranges.

The Spanish explorers became the first people to write about their overland travels in these southern regions. Modern travelers can follow their stories, and the paths they and those who came after them took, over a multitude of pleasant backroads.

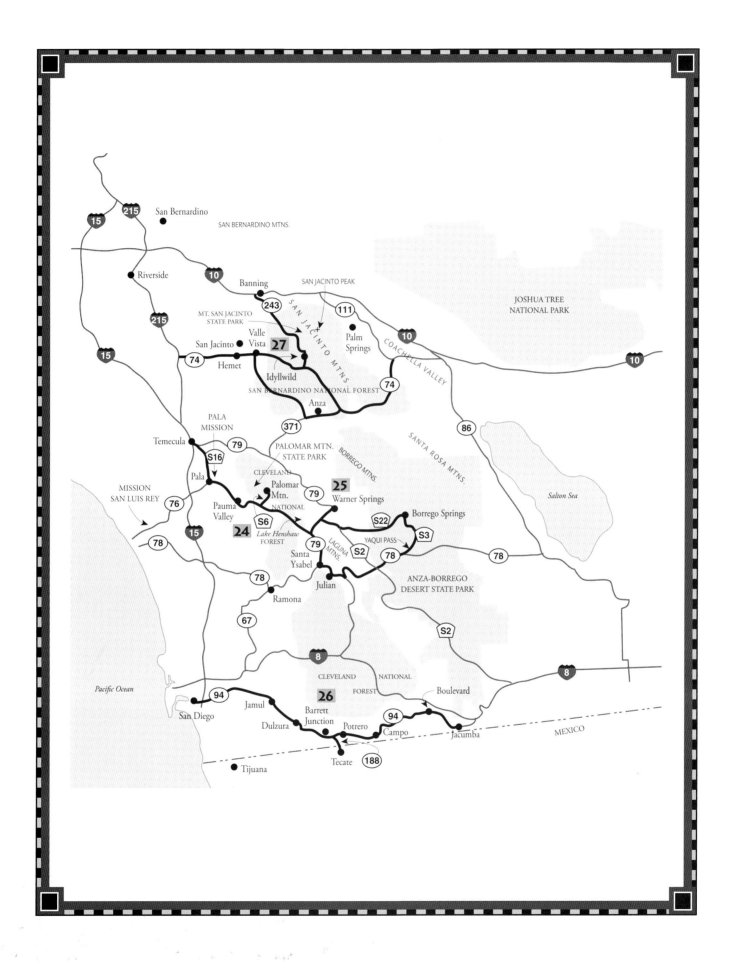

San Bernardino

SAN BERNARDINO MTNS.

JOSHUA TREE
NATIONAL PARK

Riverside

Banning

SAN JACINTO PEAK

MT. SAN JACINTO
STATE PARK

Valle
Vista

San Jacinto

Hemet

Idyllwild

SAN BERNARDINO NATIONAL FOREST

Anza

Palm
Springs

COACHELLA VALLEY

PALA
MISSION

Temecula

PALOMAR MTN.
STATE PARK

BORREGO MTNS.

SANTA ROSA MTNS.

Pala

CLEVELAND

MISSION
SAN LUIS REY

Palomar
Mtn.

NATIONAL

Pauma
Valley

Warner Springs

Borrego Springs

Salton Sea

FOREST

Lake Henshaw

YAQUI PASS

Santa
Ysabel

LAGUNA
MTNS.

ANZA-BORREGO
DESERT STATE PARK

Julian

Ramona

Pacific Ocean

CLEVELAND

NATIONAL

FOREST

Boulevard

Jamul

San Diego

Dulzura

Barrett
Junction

Potrero

Campo

Jacumba

MEXICO

Tecate

Tijuana

SAN JACINTO MTNS.

LEFT:

Orange trees are in blossom at the base of Nate Harrison Grade, which serves as an alternate, though rarely used, route from the Pauma Valley to Palomar Mountain State Park.

ABOVE:

The resort town of Julian is famous for its apple pies. The Julian Pie Company, Mom's, and Apple Alley Bakery (pictured here) are the author's favorite bakeries.

ROUTE 24

Start in Temecula, off Interstate 15. Just south of Old Town Temecula, turn south onto Pala-Temecula Road (County Road S16). Go south to Pala, then head east on California Highway 76.

Two routes lead from Highway 76 to the summit of Palomar Mountain. Where the grade of Highway 76 levels out, you can turn left onto County Road S6 (South Grade Road) and take it north to the summit. Or you can turn left onto Nate Harrison Grade and go north; Nate Harrison Grade ends at County S6, which you then follow seven miles to the summit.

From the summit, retrace your route to Highway 76, and follow it east to its junction with Highway 79. Turn left onto Highway 79 North to reach Warner Springs. Or turn right onto Highway 79 South to reach Julian.

The Laguna Mountains, rising out of the backcountry of San Diego County, are rich both in beauty and history. These mountains can easily be explored along California Highways 76 and 79 and a few adjacent backroads.

A good place to start is Old Town Temecula, which has Old West storefronts that beckon with antique stores and restaurants. At one time, the old storefronts were all there was to Temecula, but after World War II, the rural landscape around the town gave way to suburbia. Now Temecula, just off Interstate 15, serves as a bedroom community for San Diego, to the south. Housing developments chew up the rural landscape, but Old Town Temecula still displays quaint charm.

From Temecula, Highway 79 travels east along Temecula Creek. Until the early 1990s, the landscape here remained largely rural, but today the first few miles of Highway 79 run through a gauntlet of residential and commercial developments. The rural character of the land returns once the highway begins to climb out of the Temecula Valley and into the Laguna foothills.

Just east of Temecula, County Road S16 travels south to the community of Pala. Today, Pala, at the intersection of County S16 and Highway 76, is a American Indian reservation. Long ago, an American Indian village nestled at this site in the oak and scrub brush foothills, where Pala Creek enters the San Luis Rey River. The villagers called themselves the Payomkawichum, "people of the west." The Spanish called them the Luiseno and built the San Luis Rey Mission in 1798, about twenty-five miles to the west.

In 1816, the Catholic Church built the Pala Mission as a sub-mission to the Spanish mission. Pala Mission still stands, looking much as it did early in the early nineteenth century. Original native designs decorate the chapel walls; massive beams hold up the roof. The mission has a quiet courtyard, and the cemetery lies outside the thick chapel walls. Unique among the missions of California, the bell tower stands separately from the main building. The mission is different in another way: It alone continues to serve the sizeable American Indian community, while all the other California missions dating to the Spanish era have turned into museums or serve as ordinary churches.

Today, there are a few additions to the mission, including a gift shop and a museum of gemology. (A mining operation for tourmaline, a semi-precious stone, is nearby). The little Pala Market sits across the road from the mission. Part grocery store, part deli, part post office, it serves as an informal meeting place for many local residents. The tamales alone are reason for a visit.

While the Luisenos still live in and around Pala, they share the land with another tribe, the Cupenos. It was not always so. For untold centuries, the Cupenos lived in higher country to the east, around an area of hot springs in a place they called Cupa. The Spanish knew it as Agua Caliente. Although the Spanish took ownership of the land, the Cupenos continued to live and work at Cupa for more than a century. In 1892, John G. Downey, an Irish immigrant, businessman, and former governor of California, purchased land at Warner Springs and brought suit to force the Cupenos off the land.

After back and forth battles in state courts, the United States Supreme Court ruled against the Cupenos in 1901. Two years later, they were physically evicted from their ancestral home and brought to the Pala reservation. More than a century after moving to Pala, the Cupenos celebrate their heritage with the Cupa Day Celebration on the first weekend of each May. Now Cupa is little resort community known as Warner Springs, along Highway 79.

Beyond Pala, Highway 76 winds generally southeast along the course of the San Luis Rey River, through the fertile Pauma Valley. At the head of the valley, Highway 76 and the river turn east, twisting steeply up toward the flanks of Palomar Mountain. Where the grade levels out, County Road S6 takes off for Palomar Mountain State Park and the famous Palomar Observatory.

Nate Harrison Grade, climbing out of the Pauma Valley, offers an alternative route to Palomar Mountain. The mostly dirt road was named for a former slave who took up residence on the mountain. Harrison lived on the mountain for more than seventy years, offering buckets of cold spring water to passersby. Until the 1940s, when a new road was built to haul the telescope up to the observatory, Nate Harrison Grade served as the only route up the mountain.

Initially paved, Nate Harrison Grade rises above orange groves, turns to dirt, and switchbacks up the mountain. Up here, the mountain conifers and oaks have created a thick forest. Nate Harrison Grade continues through beautiful Palomar Mountain State Park as a paved road. A number of hiking trails lead out from the park, which also includes a campground, picnic areas, and a fishing pond.

Beyond the park, Nate Harrison Grade ends at County S6, which in turn travels about seven miles to the top of the mountain and ends at the Palomar Observatory. A large glass window inside the building gives a view of the massive telescope, one of the largest in the world.

From the observatory, travelers drive back down County S6, then head southeast on Highway 76 as it follows the course of the San Luis Rey River through a rugged canyon filled with oaks and sycamores. Highway 76 ends at Highway 79, a few miles past the headwaters of the river, which issue from Lake Henshaw.

Photographer Edward S. Curtis took this portrait of a Cupeno woman in 1924. The Cupenos were evicted by order of the U.S. Supreme Court from their ancestral homeland in the Laguna Mountains in 1903; they were relocated to the base of the mountains around the Pala Mission. (Courtesy of the Library of Congress)

"California possesses many of the charms that we are accustomed to associate only with certain parts of the Old World, namely: a romantic, historic background revealed in unfrequented spots unknown to the general tourist."
—Ernest Peixotto,
Romantic California, 1910

The upper portion of Nate Harrison Grade passes beneath a forest of oaks and pines.

ABOVE:

Forests, farms, and vineyards surround the little town of Julian. This farm is on Wynola Road, just north of town.

LEFT:

The Pala Mission, including its bell tower, looks much as it did when it was constructed by the Spanish in 1816.

Nate Harrison, a former Kentucky slave, settled sometime in the late nineteenth century on Palomar Mountain. The road he built—the Nate Harrison Grade—still serves as a back route up the mountain. (Courtesy of the Valley Center History Museum)

A left turn onto northbound Highway 79 leads back to Temecula. A right turn, to the south, travels past the old Santa Isabel church. Beyond Santa Isabel, Highway 79 reaches California Highway 78. Drivers can head west towards San Diego or south toward the resort town of Julian.

Julian began life as a mining camp in 1869, when gold was discovered at nearby Coleman Creek. Although the mines played out, Julian struck it rich as a resort town. The Julian Hotel, still housed in its original building, is one of the oldest continuously operating hotels in southern California. The Eagle and High Peak Mine offers guided tours of its operational gold mine. The cold winters in Julian are ideal for growing apples; the first apple trees in Julian were planted in the early 1870s. Today, folks know Julian as much for its apple pies and ciders as for its history and Old West architecture.

From Julian, roads lead east down into Anza-Borrego Desert State Park (see route 25) and south along the portion of the Laguna Mountains that were burned in the massive fires of late 2003.

DESERT SAMPLER
Anza-Borrego Desert State Park

The landscape of Anza-Borrego Desert State Park began to form three million years ago. For a long time, rain from the Pacific Ocean kept the land green. But then the Laguna and Santa Rosa Mountains rose in the west and north, cutting off the cool, moist air. The land to the east began to dry out until it became a desert.

Saber-toothed tigers, camels, miniature horses, and giant sloths once inhabited this land. As the climate changed, coyotes, bobcats, and the park's signature resident, the bighorn sheep, took the place of their prehistoric antecedents.

The park takes its name from the Spanish word for sheep, "borrego," and the name of the Spanish explorer Jaun Bautista de Anza, who pioneered an overland route from Mexico into California in 1774. Anza-Borrego is the largest state park in the contiguous United States, with some six hundred thousand acres and five hundred miles of paved and unpaved roads.

American Indian tribes, including the Kumeyaay and Cahuilla, took up residence here at least six thousand years ago, when conditions were mild. Their art—called pictographs and petroglyphs—was painted onto or picked into the desert rocks and can still be found in the park. As the land became more arid, the tribes began to migrate to the forested mountain slopes during summer, returning to the desert in winter.

Others would come: explorers like Anza, then the ranchers, and, with irrigation, farmers who settled in Borrego Valley. After World War II, developers tried to expand the community of Borrego Springs. But surrounded by the park and agricultural lands, Borrego Springs has never gown into anything more than a sleepy little resort town.

Today, visitors to Anza-Borrego are lured by the park's many natural attractions, including wildflowers, an oasis, cactus gardens, wildlife, and panoramic views of the rugged desert. Pleasant accommodations are available both in town and in two state park campgrounds.

The most comfortable time to visit the park is from November through April. The wildflower season lasts from mid March to late April. August and September bring occasional monsoon-like weather from the Gulf of California.

While exploring the entire park would take many days, a good sampling of Anza-Borrego can be made in one day. A good place to start is in Julian, the little resort town in the Laguna Mountains west of the park. California Highway 78 drops down from Julian to reach a junction with County Road S2, called Scissors Crossing for the shape of the intersection. County S2 follows the historic Butterfield Overland Mail Company stagecoach route that started in Saint Louis and ended in San Francisco; County S2 was also part of the Pony Express route. South of the junction, County S2 travels past giant cholla cactus in Mason Valley and past the trailhead

ROUTE 25

From the town of Julian in the Laguna Mountains, take California Highway 78 east into Anza-Borrego Desert State Park. Turn left onto County Road S3 and travel north to the community of Borrego Springs and the park visitor center.

To leave the park, take Montezuma Valley Road (County Road S22) west out of Borrego Springs. Follow the road to California Highway 79, leading north to Temecula or south to Julian.

> "Old history we ain't got so much of, but way back in 1774 de Anza took a short cut through this here Borego Desert on his march to the Pacific."
> —Harry Oliver,
> *Desert Rough Cuts*, 1938

A hedgehog cactus, so named because it grows in tight clumps, blooms on the roof garden at the Anza-Borrego Desert State Park visitor center.

The odd-looking ocotillo plant begins to sprout leaves as soon as it rains.

California fan palms, the only palms native to the western United States, appear to stand in formation at the oasis in Borrego-Palm Canyon.

This hut in the desert was photographed by Edward S. Curtis in 1924. The Cahuilla and other tribes lived in the desert during the winter and moved into the Laguna Mountains during the summer. (Courtesy of the Library of Congress)

in Blair Valley that leads to American Indian rock art.

But our route continues east of Scissors Crossing on Highway 78. The highway follows San Felipe Creek past the Sentenac Cienega (Spanish for "swamp"), a vast marshland that runs down Sentenac Canyon. Where the marsh ends, the true desert begins. The weird ocotillo, a spiny, spindly tree that looks like a refugee from a science fiction film, begins to dot the sides of the canyon.

The highway reaches a junction with County Road S3, where travelers will find twenty-three tree-shaded sites at the comfortable Tamarisk Grove Campground. A trailhead across the road from the campground begins a one-mile loop that leads past several cactus varieties and is a good place to look for bighorn sheep.

About a mile beyond the campground on County S3, Yaqui Pass offers sweeping views south to the San Felipe Wash and north into Borrego Valley. The deeply eroded mud hills of the Borrego Badlands to the north become visible, too. The rugged Santa Rosa Mountains rise above the badlands.

Just over ten miles north of Yaqui Pass lies the town of Borrego Springs. The Kiwanis Club sells bags of grapefruit at a self-service booth located on the town's signature "Christmas Circle," a traffic circle that also serves as the town's municipal park.

The Borrego-Palm Canyon Campground is just west of town, at the base of the Laguna Mountains. The park's visitor center, near the campground, was built partially underground to conserve heat in the winter and stay cool in the summer. A few steps up to the roof lead to a flower and cactus garden. Desert pupfish swim in a small pool in front of the building.

From the upper end of the campground, where there is a second pupfish pond, a 1.5-mile hike leads to an oasis of native palm trees. During winter and spring, a twenty-five–foot tall waterfall tumbles into the oasis. This site is another good place to watch for bighorn sheep, which sometimes clamber on ledges above the oasis.

When it's time to leave the park, Montezuma Valley Road (County Road S22) offers a quick route up an exceedingly steep grade into the mountains to eventually meet the northern end of County Road S2; beyond this junction is California Highway 79, leading north to Temecula or south to Julian.

Before leaving Anza-Borrego, it is worth a stop at the viewpoint at the top of the grade, almost fifteen hundred feet above the desert floor. This is the place to say farewell to the park. The wildflowers, oasis, cactus gardens, and wildlife may be all but invisible from this elevation. But the loss of the desert's details is more than offset by the panorama of the colorful landscape, stretching from green grapefruit groves in Borrego Springs to the yellow-brown Borrego Badlands and all the way out, on a clear day, to the blue Salton Sea on the edge of the horizon.

JAMUL TO JACUMBA
Highway 94 and the Inland Empire

To travel through the foothills of the Laguna Mountains one hundred years ago, most travelers took the stagecoach from San Diego. The stage departed in the morning from the Commercial Hotel, a few blocks from the harbor. It took the better part of the day to reach the community of Campo, which served as an important connecting point between California, Arizona, and Mexico. Today, the mode of transportation into the whimsically named Mountain Empire may be more modern and the journey far swifter, but much of the landscape remains unchanged in this scenic and most southern region of California.

The best route into the Mountain Empire is along California Highway 94. The first nineteen miles extend from San Diego into the Laguna foothills over a four-lane freeway. The highway narrows to two lanes at Jamul, a semi-rural community that has endured the march of housing tracts and the rise of shopping malls. Jamul, a American Indian word, is said to mean "the place where antelope go to drink water."

From San Diego, follow California Highway 94 east to Jamul. Continue twenty miles east on Highway 94, then take a two-mile side trip on California Highway 188 South to the Mexican city of Tecate. Back on Highway 94, continue east to Boulevard. From Boulevard, take Old California Highway 80 seven miles southeast to Jacumba. Beyond Jacumba, Old Highway 80 reaches Interstate 8; go west back to San Diego or east to the Sonora Desert.

The Gaskill Brothers Store in Campo Valley was designed like a fortress, after the original wood structure was attacked by bandits in a famous 1875 shootout. Today, the Stone Store is a museum containing exhibits about the history of the Mountain Empire. This photograph, taken about 1887, shows Silas Gaskill standing next to the horse. (Courtesy of the San Diego Historical Society)

Pickup trucks slowly fade in the California sun at Campo's Motor Transport Museum. The museum contains an enormous collection of antique trucks dating to the early twentieth century, as well as memorabilia and literature about the history of the transportation industry in the United States.

California Highway 94 runs through pretty Potrero Valley. (Potrero is the Spanish word for horse corral.) The southernmost campground in California is here, too, in Potrero Regional Park.

The Motor Transport Museum sits on the former property of the Campo Feldspar Mill, which produced porcelain for bathroom fixtures and spark plugs.

In this semi-arid landscape of gently rolling hills, the summers can be hot, but the winters are mild. The vegetation is thick with plants like the red-barked manzanita. Scrub oaks usually grow no higher than fifteen feet. Stately oaks and cottonwoods grow in the canyon and valley bottoms where seasonal creeks and rivers provide enough water.

Highway 94 continues past the rustic little communities of Dulzura, Engineer Springs, Barrett Junction, and Potrero, all located in valleys pleasantly green in winter and spring. Cleveland National Forest and higher country lies to the north, while the Mexican border is just to the south.

California Highway 188, all two miles of it, takes travelers to the town of Tecate, just south of the border. Invisible from Highway 94, Tecate is not a major tourist destination. Unlike crossings in Tijuana, south of San Diego, the wait to cross the border at Tecate in either direction is minimal. The town's quiet plaza and business district spread across a valley; its homes cling to slopes of the surrounding hills. While the U.S. side of the border is lightly populated, Tecate, has more than fifty thousand residents.

Past Highway 188, Highway 94 continues about ten miles to Campo, a rural community situated in a pleasant valley dotted with oaks. It is home to three museums. The Motor Transport Museum features a collection of antique trucks, plus memorabilia and literature about the American transportation industry. The San Diego Railroad Museum dedicates itself to preserving the history of the rails in the southwest; the museum runs excursion trains on weekends. The Gaskill Brothers' Stone Store Museum houses exhibits about the history of the Mountain Empire. One exhibit tells about nearby Camp Lockett, where the last of an elite, all-black cavalry unit, the famed Buffalo Soldiers, were quartered. Until they were disbanded during the opening years of World War II, the Buffalo Soldiers guarded the border and the San Diego and Arizona Railroad.

The Stone Store was built by the Gaskill brothers, Silas and Lumen. Silas crossed the Great Plains to reach California in 1850, and his brother Lumen traveled by ship around Cape Horn and South America to San Francisco seven years later. After working as miners and bear hunters, the brothers settled in Campo Valley in 1868. The Gaskills eventually owned much of the land in the valley. They operated a blacksmith shop and stables and built a store over Campo Creek. To keep perishables cool, the brothers lowered them through a trapdoor into the creek water. Lumen recorded the store's business in a ledger, in which he also noted numerous home remedies and household tips, such as how to "Break a Dog from Sucking Eggs."

The Gaskills' success brought them to the attention of Cruz Lopez, otherwise known as Pancho, an outlaw who lived across the border in Tecate. The brothers received a tip that Lopez and his gang planned to rob the store. When Lopez and his men rode up on the morning of December 4, 1875, the Gaskills were ready with six double-barreled shotguns strate-

> *"take a 1/2 Sheet of Brown Paper & twist it up like a lamp liter & place the small End in the Cavity in the tooth then Set the other End a fire & hold it in as long as Posibal."*
> —Lumen Gaskill, 1880s ledger entry on how to cure a toothache

gically placed around the store and their stables. In the ensuing shootout, six of the seven bandits were killed. Both brothers were wounded but survived. The story went out by telegraph, and the battle became part of the lore of the Old West.

Later, the store was torn down, and the Gaskills replaced it with fortress-like building that now houses the Stone Store Museum.

Highway 94 continues another fifteen miles through gently rolling foothills to the community of Boulevard, where it joins Interstate 8 for a quick return to San Diego. But a trip into the Mountain Empire should be extended from Boulevard along scenic Old Highway 80 to include the community of Jacumba, seven miles east.

Jacumba was once a popular hot springs resort; according to local legend, movie actor Clark Gable was a regular in the 1930s. The shell of an old resort slowly crumbles on the west side of town. A new resort, less opulent than the old one, shares space in town with a market and gift shop and not much more. Beyond Jacumba, the highway almost touches the border with Mexico before it reaches Interstate 8, where travelers have a choice to return west to the San Diego area or begin yet another backroad adventure eastward into the Sonora Desert.

WELCOME TO RAMONALAND
The San Jacinto Mountains

The peoples who entered the San Jacinto Mountains over the centuries brought along their histories and their myths. These stories sometimes mixed together, blurring the line between reality and legend. The backroads around these mountains let travelers explore these stories up close.

The most famous story to emerge from the San Jacinto Mountains comes from Helen Hunt Jackson. Although little known today, Jackson was an important writer in the late nineteenth century. She turned to a writing career after the deaths of her first husband and her two children, becoming the most prominent American woman writer of her day.

After traveling to Southern California and the San Jacinto Mountains, Jackson wrote her most enduring work, *Ramona*. Published in 1884, the book is a Victorian-era romance about the doomed love of Ramona and Alessandro, who vainly try to find freedom in the San Jacinto Mountains. *Ramona* is also an allegory about prejudice and injustice directed by whites against the Mission Indians of Southern California. Both in Jackson's time and today, American Indians from Los Angeles south to the Mexican border are known as Mission Indians, because they descend from the people evangelized by the Spanish friars in the late eighteenth and early nineteenth centuries.

Jackson based her book on the real-life murder of Juan Diego, a Cahuilla man, by a white man. Diego's murder was witnessed by his wife. Her real name has been lost to history, but after Jackson's book, she be-

ROUTE 27

From Interstate 215, take California Highway 74 east to Valle Vista.

To reach the mountain resort town of Idyllwild, continue east on Highway 74, then head north on California Highway 243. From Idyllwild, drive north on Highway 243 to reach Interstate 10 at the town of Banning.

For a more remote backroad through a wild canyon, head south in Valle Vista on Fairview Road. This road changes names to Bautista Canyon Road; follow it south to California Highway 371, just west of Anza. To reach the Coachella Valley, drive east on Highway 371, then head northeast on Highway 74.

ABOVE:

Built in the early twentieth century, Jacumba's "Chinese Castle" reputedly has its own hot spring inside the house, used to soothe the aches and pains of the original owners. Built by a doctor for his wife, who was from China, the house was later used by the U.S. Army to treat soldiers who had been exposed to mustard gas in World War I.

RIGHT:

An old tractor rusts along California Highway 94, not far from Campo Valley.

A sycamore tree grows alongside Highway 94. The scenic rural landscape east of Jamul draws visitors to southern California's whimsically named Mountain Empire.

came Ramona. Today, the remote area of the San Jacinto foothills where the murder occurred is known as Juan Diego Flats.

Jackson hoped, as she wrote to a friend, that her book would "set forth some Indian experiences in a way to move people's hearts." The book did move people. It literally brought thousands of admirers to Southern California and "Ramonaland." They visited "Ramona's Birthplace" in the town of San Gabriel as well her "Marriage Place" in Old Town in San Diego. Tourists were introduced to several "real" Ramonas. Some people were said to be disappointed when they learned the book was a work of fiction.

"The jagged top and spurs of San Jacinto Mountain shone like the turrets and posterns of a citadel built of rubies."
—Helen Hunt Jackson,
Ramona, 1884

The true land of Ramona is not that difficult to explore. The San Jacinto Mountains make up a relatively compact range, easy to circumnavigate in a day, although more leisurely explorations beckon along the backroads. The quickest way into the San Jacintos from San Diego or Los Angeles is over California Highway 74, east of Interstate 215. Highway 74 travels east through the San Jacinto Valley, through the town of Hemet. Past the community of Valle Vista, the highway climbs the flanks of Mount San Jacinto and crosses into the San Bernardino National Forest. There, it reaches a junction with California Highway 243, which leads up toward the picturesque and pleasant resort town of Idyllwild.

Tucked deep in an evergreen forest, Idyllwild sits a mile above sea level. Nearby are various trailheads to Mount San Jacinto, rising above the surrounding mountains at 10,805 feet above sea level. The mountain's rather isolated summit offers panoramic views over much of southern California. Idyllwild is also close to several campgrounds. Nearby, rock climbers scale the massive granite outcroppings of Taquitz and Suicide Rocks, two of southern California's favorite climbing destinations. The renowned Idyllwild Arts Foundation conducts programs in dance, theater, creative writing, music and the visual arts.

North of Idyllwild, scenic Highway 243 begins to zigzag its way down the gigantic northwest flanks of the San Jacinto Mountains. The pines give way to oaks and finally to chaparral and massive outcrops of white granite. With the towering San Bernardino Mountains to the north, Highway 243 reaches Interstate 10 at the town of Banning. To reach the base of the Palm Springs Aerial Tram, take Interstate 10 east about eleven miles, then exit onto California Highway 111 and follow it east another ten miles. The tram travels two and a half miles up Mount San Jacinto to a chalet, picnic area, and trails into San Jacinto State Park and Wilderness. To visit downtown Palm Springs, the popular desert resort town also at the base of Mount San Jacinto, continue a half mile east along Highway 111 past the turnoff to the tram station.

Another way to reach the desert from Idyllwild is to backtrack south on Highway 243 from Banning. Drive east on Highway 74 and explore the

San Jacintos on their southern and eastern flanks. Along the way the route travels past pine forests and immense mountain meadows, spur roads leading to various trail heads, and Lake Hemet, with its own campground and a boat launch. Beyond its junction with California Highway 371, Highway 74 begins its descent into the Coachella Valley, ending at the city of Palm Desert. Palm Springs is about 15 miles to the west. The entire run from Banning to Palm Desert, over Highways 74 and 243, is known as the Palms to Pines Highway.

An alternate route into the San Jacintos begins just east of Valle Vista. It follows in reverse the route taken in 1774 by the Juan Bautista de Anza expedition that pioneered an overland route from Mexico to San Francisco. It begins on Fairview Road, which quickly becomes Bautista Canyon Road. A dusty eight-mile stretch of dirt road passes through the San Bernardino National Forest to travel through a wide canyon that looks as wild as it did when Anza rode through it more than two centuries ago.

The head of the canyon ends at California Highway 371. The reservation for the Cahuilla Band of Mission Indians is just west of Highway 371, in the broad, still largely rural Anza Valley. Highway 79, which leads to Temecula and Interstate 15, is about 15 miles to the west. About six miles east of Bautista Canyon Road, Highway 371 ends at Highway 74, the Palms to Pines Highway.

Helen Hunt Jackson died at age fifty-five, less than a year after the publication of *Ramona*. She worried that readers enjoyed the book more for its story than its message. Had she lived longer, Jackson would have known that *Ramona* did help stir public opinion about the plight of American Indians.

Ramona mixed real and imaginary stories to create a myth of old southern California. The people of the cities of Hemet and San Jacinto honor that myth each spring. The book, beautifully transformed, has become the acclaimed Ramona Pageant, California's official outdoor play. With a cast of hundreds of local residents—only the two leading roles are cast for professionals—*Ramona* has been staged almost every year since 1923 in a natural amphitheater south of Hemet. As Jackson hoped, Ramona's story about love and freedom still has the power "to move people's hearts."

Ramona is the official outdoor pageant of California. It has been staged almost every year since 1923 in a natural amphitheater in the town of Hemet. More than four hundred local residents take part in the play. The first production is pictured here. (Courtesy of Phil Brigandi)

Taquitz Rock towers over the resort town of Idyllwild. The massive granite outcropping is a favorite destination of rock climbers.

The Palms to Pines Highway travels from the desert into the San Jacinto and Santa Rosa Mountains, and back to the desert. The landscape pictured here is above the city of Indian Wells.

INDEX

Bicyclists pedal up Schueren Road toward Stunt Road and the crest of the Santa Monica Mountains. A panoramic view of Santa Monica Bay will reward their efforts.

FURTHER READING

Caughey, John and Laree. *California Heritage — An Anthology of History and Literature*. Los Angeles: Ward Ritchie Press, 1962.

Crawford, Richard W. *Stranger Than Fiction: Vignettes of San Diego History*. San Diego: San Diego Historical Society, 1995

Donley, Michael W. *Atlas of California*. Culver City, Calif.: Pacific Book Center, 1979.

Fletcher, Colin. *The Thousand-Mile Summer*. Berkeley: Howell-North Books, 1964.

James, George Wharton. *Through Ramona's Country*. Boston: Little, Brown and Co., 1913.

Jenkins, J. C. and Ruby. *Exploring the Southern Sierra: West Side*. Berkeley: Wilderness Press, 1995.

Kyle, Douglas E. *Historic Spots in California*. Stanford: Stanford University Press, 1990.

Newmark, Harris. *Sixty Years in Southern California, 1853–1913*. Los Angeles: Zeitlin and Aver Brugge, 1970.

Schoenherr, Allan A. *A Natural History of California*. Berkeley: University of California Press, 1990.

Wheeler, Gordon B. *Black California: A History of African-Americans in the Golden State*. New York: Hippocrene Books, 1993.

ABOUT THE AUTHOR

David M. Wyman has searched the backroads of California for stories and photographs since 1970, when he wrote a travel column for his college newspaper. A freelance writer and photographer based in Los Angeles, Dave owns a photo tour company that conducts trips throughout California and the southwest. He earned a graduate degree in journalism from UCLA and directed the travel photography and wilderness outings programs at the University of Southern California. Dave's work has appeared in *Outdoor Photographer*, *Outside*, *Sierra*, and other national magazines. He is the author and photographer of *Backroads of Northern California*, published by Voyageur Press.

Dave's choice of photographic equipment includes Minolta and Canon digital cameras, Pentax and Olympus 35mm film cameras, and his mother's 1956 Rolleiflex medium-format film camera.

ACKNOWLEDGMENTS

Although the title page lists me as the author and photographer of this book, I had the help and support of many people. First and foremost, I want to thank my wife, Kathy Burke, for allowing me to wander to my heart's content over the southern half of the Golden State in search of photographs and stories. At home, we usually have a rule against reading during meals, but Kathy, and my daughters Rebecca and Nora, were always willing to listen to me read early versions of the text over dinner.

My wife was also my travel companion on several trips for the book. When Kathy wasn't with me, my good friend Reid Bogert often as not was. An avid photographer, Reid helped me find many photographs that appear in this book. Photographers Bob Bernardo, Dave Welling, and Winn Krafton performed similar duties for me.

Lori Sweeny generously edited most of the text before I submitted it to my publisher, saving me much time and later embarrassment. Kate Dumont and Irene Shibata also helped with early editing. Irene traveled with me on some of my photography excursions and supplied me with hot coffee and homemade cookies.

State Parks Ranger Bill Moffet did double duty: He helped me explore and photograph the San Joaquin Valley tule elk reserve and supplied me with photographs of Colonel Allen Allensworth, founder of California's first black colony. Others who helped me secure historical images include Bruce Petty, Marcia Stout, Blair Davenport, Bob Graham, Marc Wannamaker, Sharon Moore, Ollie Fiscalini, Petei McHenry, Thomas Featherstone, Tina McDowell, Helen Cowan, and Chris Travers. Rick Crawford kindly allowed me to use a quote from his fascinating book, *Stranger Than Fiction: Vignettes of San Diego History*.

Local guides, historians, naturalists, and raconteurs who kept me pointed in the right direction include Gary Valenzuela, Kamme Osborn, Glenn Harris, Paul and Virginia de Fonville, Dolores Rossbeck, Donald Storm, Victoria Duarte, Suzanne Jones, Lynda and Rory O'Toole, Tom Ratican, Debra Hodkin, Jane Strong, Robert Harris, H. R. Slater, and Dr. Jim Cornett.

Voyageur Press trusted me to complete a second pictorial travel guide that would fairly represent almost seventy-five thousand square miles of California, stretching from the center of the state to the Mexican border. That task, while at times difficult to execute, was extremely satisfying when completed. Thanks are particularly due to my editor, Danielle Ibister.

Backroads of Southern California and its predecessor, *Backroads of Northern California*, would not exist without the support of Dave Anderson, who believed my California photographs deserved a wider audience and who worked on my behalf to make that happen.

I don't want to overlook the effect a television program, *Route 66*, had on me in the early 1960s. That legendary show followed the fictional adventures of Buzz Murdoch and Todd Stiles (played by actors George Maharis and Martin Milner). Todd and Buzz were young men who drove around the United States in a Corvette, trying to earn a living while learning about life and love. While I have never been lucky enough to own a Corvette, I have, like Todd and Buzz, enjoyed many adventures while traveling along the backroads of California.